The Danger of Self-Love

THE DANGER OF SELF LOVE

PAUL BROWNBACK

MOODY PRESS
CHICAGO

All Scripture quotations in this book are from the *New American Standard Bible,* © 1960, 1962, 1963, 1968, 1971, 1972, 1973, 1975, and 1977 by The Lockman Foundation, and are used by permission.

Material taken from *You're Someone Special* by Bruce Narramore, © 1978 by Zondervan Publishing House is used by permission of Zondervan Publishing House.

Material taken from "Is Self-Love Biblical?" by John Piper, *Christianity Today,* 12 August 1977, © 1977 by *Christianity Today* is used by permission.

Library of Congress Cataloging in Publication Data

Brownback, Paul
  The danger of self-love.

  Includes bibliographical references.
  1. Self-love (Theology) 2. Existential psychology. 3. Humanistic psychology. 4. Christianity—Psychology. I. Title.
BV4639.B83 1982   248.4   82-12543
ISBN 0-8024-2068-0

6 7 8 9 10 11 12 Printing/LC/Year 94 93 92 91 90 89

Printed in the United States of America

To Connie — a vivid reflection
of other-oriented living

Contents

Preface

The first time I heard the concept of self-love presented as a Christian virtue I had strong reservations about the idea, and substantial study over the past twelve years has only deepened that concern. Why? From beginning to end the focus of Scripture is the exaltation of God and not man. "But God has chosen the foolish things of the world to shame the wise, and God has chosen the weak things of the world to shame the things which are strong, and the base things of the world and the despised, God has chosen, the things that are not, that He might nullify the things that are, that no man should boast before God. . . . That, just as it is written, 'Let him who boasts, boast in the Lord' " (1 Corinthians 1:27-29, 31).

What I was hearing from the advocates of self-love seemed to me to be opposed to this flow of Scripture. It appeared that Psalm 139:14 was virtually being rewritten to read "I will praise *me*, for I am fearfully and wonderfully made." So my involvement in this subject was born out of a need to know whether ideas that seemed so opposite could really be put together in a Christian world view.

My study soon revealed that little serious exegetical/ theological work had been done on the subject. Although much had been written, almost all of it touched only lightly on the exegetical and theological problems connected with self-love. For example, an attempt at a careful biblical definition of love was almost universally lacking. In addition, Paul's designation of self-love as a prime characteristic of the evil of the last days (2 Timothy 3) had been given practically no consideration at all.

The lack of work in those and other areas has prompted this volume. It does not claim to be an in-depth study of all the issues, but it is offered with the hope that what is presented is sufficient to provide Christians with an accurate analysis of the contemporary theory of self-love in light of the Word of God. Most importantly, it seeks to provide a biblical alternative.

In the process we have wrestled with many concepts, arguments, and ideas. But ideas are related to the people who formulate and propagate them. It has been our objective to dissect and criticize *ideas*, not the *people* related to them. If in the midst of grappling with issues it appears to be otherwise, it should be noted that that was not our intent.

This book would never have been begun apart from the encouragement of my wife, and it certainly would not have been completed without the long hours she spent at the typewriter. Much of the research was done in conjunction with a dissertation for New York University. I am deeply indebted to Prof. Norma Thompson for her encouragement and valuable advice. A special word of thanks is also due my parents for their help with the expenses involved in this undertaking. I also want to express my appreciation to the board of directors of Citadel Bible College for giving me the freedom and encouragement to work on this project.

Paul Brownback

1

Some Initial Concerns

My class looked at me in utter disbelief. I knew it was coming. That statement always brought the same reaction from college students. "Do you really mean it? When you were a boy, there was no television?!"

I cannot remember when television first became a reality for the general public, but my first recollection dates back to when I was about ten. The local firehouse was the first place in the neighborhood to own a television set, and we used to make weekly visits to actually see the Lone Ranger doing the things we had previously only heard about on radio. Not long after that, the big boom came and almost every family had to have its own set.

Of course the students had no problem imagining that I was that old. From their perspective, my personal history extended back to infinity past, even though I only predated them by about twenty years. Their struggle was in grasping the idea that life existed before television. Though they knew objectively that there were such times, trying to fathom what that kind of world would be like was another story. And to have a live representative from that pristine era verify its reality was especially shocking!

No doubt many Christians would react the same way today, if they were told that the popular ideas of self-love, self-esteem, the Christian's need for a positive self-image, and a parent's responsibility to develop his child's self-worth were not prominent concerns for the informed believer of even ten years ago. "What! A day when self-regard was not a major aspect of Christian living? How did Christians make it? Were they maladjusted?"

One student from a highly respected seminary told me that one of his professors once suggested that the apostle Paul might have been better adjusted if he had had the advantage of contemporary Christian insights on self-love. Apparently this professor was experiencing the same struggles in attempting to conceive of an era without a focus on self-love.

A NEW CONCERN FOR CHRISTIANS

Though it may seem surprising, the fact is that little more than a decade ago this topic was virtually unheard of in evangelical circles. A look at the copyright page of some of the more prominent volumes on the subject (many of which will be cited in this book) reveals the significant fact that the earliest date among them is 1974. It was about that time or perhaps slightly before that the Christian public's awareness of self-love was born.

Since the evangelical preoccupation with the teaching of self-love has not yet celebrated its tenth birthday, the reader should be able to recall the days when such an emphasis did not exist in popular evangelical thinking. Why then do we have such difficulty in imagining such a day? Probably because the concept of self-love has been so immediately, enthusiastically, and unreservedly received by evangelicals that it has become a part of us. "Self-love" became a household term virtually overnight. It was a vivid occurrence of love at first sight. This concept and Christian thinking skipped the engagement period and were joined in a very sudden marriage. The result is that since about 1974 the Christian market has been flooded with literature on the subject. And its propagation has not been restricted to the printed page. It seems that every sermon and evangelical seminar had to include some teaching on the Christian's spiritual obligation to feel good about himself.

John Piper portrays the enthusiastic reception given to self-love by lamenting:

> Today the first and greatest commandment is, "Thou shalt love thyself." And the explanation for almost every interpersonal problem is thought to lie in someone's low self-esteem. Sermons, articles, and books have pushed this idea into the Christian mind. It is a rare congregation, for example, that does not stumble over the "vermicular theology" of Isaac Watts's "Alas! And Did My Saviour Bleed": "Would He devote that sacred head/For such a worm as I?"[1]

John R. W. Stott expressed it this way: "A chorus of many voices is chanting in unison today that I must at all costs love myself. . . ."[2]

This sudden escalation of teaching on self-love should not be viewed as a mere promotional campaign aimed at getting the evangelical public to buy a new product. Rather it was the spontaneous response of those who were firmly convinced of the solid biblical basis of self-love. And, as we have noted, almost immediately the Christian public felt warmly at home with its newfound friend; self-love has been easily incorporated into the mind-set of evangelical Christians.

All one needs to do to verify this is to walk into his Sunday school class next Sunday morning and ask, "Should a Christian love himself?" He probably will discover quickly that the tide of opinion flows strongly toward a positive response. The interesting discovery this kind of informal research uncovers is that people have not

1. John Piper, "Is Self-Love Biblical?" *Christianity Today*, 12 August 1977, p. 6.
2. John R. W. Stott, "Must I Really Love Myself?" *Christianity Today*, 5 May 1978, p. 34.

only adopted self-love theory in breadth, but also in depth, that is, there is usually an extremely strong emotional tie to the concept. It has become a cardinal doctrine in the minds of many, a part of orthodoxy in the practical sense of the word. The marriage between self-love theory and the evangelical Christian has in fact been consummated. That is why it is difficult for us to relate to a day when self-love was not a prevalent theme in our preaching, teaching, and writing.

A POPULAR THEME IN PSYCHOLOGY

Though self-love is relatively new to the evangelical world, it is not a new idea. It was a prominent theme in secular psychology in the 1940s, coming to full bloom in the '50s and '60s. As we shall seek to demonstrate, the evangelical adoption of the secular theory of self-love was with very few revisions. A number of evangelical writers mention in passing that secular psychologists such as Carl Rogers have inspired their thoughts regarding self-love, but few go into detail regarding the nature or extent of that relationship.

We have been using the term *self-love*, but a number of other terms are used interchangeably by evangelicals and most secular authors to refer to this phenomenon: "self-esteem," "positive self-image," "self-regard," and "self-worth" are some of the more common designations used. There are also descriptive phrases such as "feeling good about yourself," "liking yourself," "being fond of yourself," and so on. Those terms are almost always used without distinction. For example, seldom if ever do you find an evangelical writer saying, "By *self-love* I mean concept *A*, but *self-esteem* refers to idea *B*," though an author may prefer one term to another because he feels it communicates the concept more clearly.

Self-love means simply that a person has a positive attitude about himself, feels good about himself. That is, when a person thinks about himself he has a positive emotional response. Self-love, then, is basically an emotion or attitude.

Self-love theory begins with the assertion that large segments of society are suffering from a low self-image or lack of self-love. Often this is said to be a special problem among evangelical Christians because of the stress on the depravity of man in evangelical theology. This deficiency is seen to have devastating consequences for both the individual and society. The individual suffers from anxiety, fear, feelings of rejection, and a host of other maladies. Those symptoms produce consequences such as a lack of productivity at work and failure in marriage and other interpersonal relationships.

James Dobson speaks about the social by-products of low self-esteem:

> The matter of personal worth is not only the concern of those who lack it. In a real sense, the health of an entire society depends on the ease with which the individual members gain personal acceptance. *Thus, whenever the keys to self-esteem are seemingly out of reach for a large percentage of the people, as in twentieth-century America, then widespread "mental illness," neuroticism, hatred, alcoholism, drug abuse, violence, and social disorder will certainly occur"* [emphasis his].[3]

Dobson sees a cause/effect relationship between a lack of self-acceptance and the worst personal and social problems of our times.

Not only is low self-esteem viewed as a plague to the individual and society, but the converse is also affirmed to be true. A healthy self-image is the source of an abundance of blessing, the foundation for personal well-being and happiness, and a well-adjusted life. It is the basis of

3. James Dobson, *Hide or Seek* (Old Tappan, N.J.: Revell, 1974), pp. 12-13.

productivity, the catalyst for meaningful interpersonal relationships, and the means by which we make our best contribution to society. Walter Trobisch, in *Love Yourself*, quotes with apparent approval a Catholic philosopher, Romano Guardini: "The act of self-acceptance is the root of all things."[4] So, at the root of all major personal and social ills is a poor self-image or lack of self-acceptance, and the means of success, the "root of all things," is self-love.

There is another aspect of self-love that adds to its significance. It is seen to be Christian. Loving yourself is a biblical thing to do. Jesus calls us to love our neighbor as ourselves (Matthew 22:39), so it appears that Scripture is declaring self-love to be a prerequisite to neighbor-love. This biblical blessing on the concept is of special importance since, as we shall see, the historical roots of self-theory are traced back not to Christian theology but rather to secular psychology. A declaration such as that found in the "neighbor passage" appears to demonstrate that self-love is indeed a biblical teaching, and that its recent discovery by secular psychology (or at least its popularization and the discovery of its profound and far-reaching implications) should be viewed simply as another example of the maxim that "all truth is God's truth." We as Christians should be grateful that the secular world has brought this truth to our attention.

By now the reader probably realizes that this book does not share the view that the contemporary self-love revolution among evangelicals is nothing but the happy rediscovery of a clear scriptural precept. To examine this teaching carefully is the nature of the task at hand. We have already noted the popularity that self-love enjoys among Christians and the zeal with which many hold this concept. In light of that, to get the reader over the initial shock of the suggestion that self-love may not be a

4. Walter Trobisch, *Love Yourself* (Downers Grove: Inter-Varsity, 1976), p. 9.

thoroughly biblical concept is perhaps the hardest step. Once that is accomplished and we can turn to an objective evaluation of the matter, the really difficult part may already be behind us.

In order to help accomplish this, I want to sketch in a preliminary way some of the reasons I believe a Christian should be cautious about the concept of self-love; why he should look twice before he leaps.

REASONS FOR CAUTION

Our first concern is that this area of study is relatively new to evangelical Christianity. That in itself does not prove it to be right or wrong. It does mean, though, that it is untested—years of trial give an experience factor, yield a data base, a broad literature. Those are lacking in the study of self-love; therefore, there is cause to proceed with caution. We are familiar with cases in which a new drug comes on the market and is readily accepted, only to prove several years later to have serious side effects. Perhaps we have yet to see all of the effects of self-love on the evangelical world.

THE CONCEPT IN CHURCH HISTORY

Church literature. The matter of newness raises a second item of concern. Self-love has not been held and taught historically by the church. Little can be found in the history of church literature that supports self-love as it is taught today. Of the scattered references we do find, a closer examination often brings to light one of two difficulties. Either the author was not referring to the type of self-love advocated today, or his theology was questionable. An example of the latter is Meister Eckhart, a German mystic who died in 1327. He advocated self-love, but he also had tendencies toward pantheism. He believed that saved men became divinity. It is one thing to be a partaker of the divine nature (2 Peter 1:4) and another to become God. The fact is that few if any theologically sound men in the past eras of church history have advocated the type of self-love that is espoused today.

On the contrary, there has been much written in the annals of the church that reflects a conflict between self-love and Christian thought. As early as St. Augustine we find that current flowing strongly. In *The City of God* he states, "Two cities have been formed by two loves; the earthly by the love of self, even to the contempt of God, the heavenly by the love of God even to the contempt of self. The former, in a word, glories in itself, the latter in the Lord."[5] The same basic thrust may be found in each age of the church and in various branches of orthodox theology. This negative attitude of the church toward self-love is even noted by some secular proponents of the theory. Erich Fromm called John Calvin "a pest" because of the derogatory pronouncements on the subject found in his *Institutes of the Christian Religion.* Calvin observed, "For so blindly do we all rush in the direction of self-love that everyone thinks he has a good reason for exalting himself and despising all others in comparison."[6] He then offers a cure for the problem:

> For there is no other remedy than to pluck up by the roots those most noxious pests, self-love and love of victory *(philoneikia kai philautia).* This the doctrine of Scripture does. For it teaches us to remember, that the endowments which God has bestowed upon us are not our own, but His free gifts, and that those who plume themselves upon them betray their ingratitude.[7]

5. Augustine *Civitas Dei* XIV, 28. Cited by John Warwick Montgomery, *The Shape of the Past* (Minneapolis: Bethany Fellowship, 1975), p. 46.
6. John Calvin, *Institutes of the Christian Religion,* trans. Henry Beveridge, 2 vols. (Grand Rapids: Eerdmans, 1966), 2:10.
7. Ibid.

As we develop the concept of self-love we will see that from every indication Calvin is objecting to the kind of self-love encouraged today. Not only do we not find self-love espoused in historical evangelical literature, but we find it condemned. The illustrations given are only a small sampling of the general attitude of God's people in past generations toward the idea that we must love ourselves.

Hymnology. Another place this negative attitude toward self-love becomes apparent is in hymnology. We have already noted Piper's mention of the struggle that self-love proponents have with "At The Cross." Anthony Hoekema rejoices that some hymnals now delete "my own worthlessness" from the last line of "Beneath The Cross of Jesus."[8] But that is just the beginning of the hymnological sorrows for the self-love enthusiast. In the same hymn the words "my sinful self, my only shame" no doubt do nothing to endear themselves to self-love advocates. The fact is that a substantial amount of ink would be needed to line out all the pronouncements of the hymn writers that are out of sympathy with self-love theory. It seems, then, that the heart of historical Christianity as expressed in its hymns flows contrary to the doctrine of self-love.

We readily acknowledge that general opposition to a concept throughout church history does not necessarily make it wrong, but when a number of church leaders agree on a subject such as this, we cannot help but ask why. It could be because they saw exegetical and theological problems with self-love that for some reason have been overlooked in our day. It should be a concern to us as evangelicals that such giants of the faith stand against us on a major theological issue. That in itself is sufficient cause for an in-depth study of the issue.

The lives of great Christians. The aversion to the idea of self-love throughout the history of the church is trou-

8. Anthony A. Hoekema, *The Christian Looks at Himself* (Grand Rapids: Eerdmans, 1975), p. 16.

blesome on another count. As we study the lives of great
saints in past ages we often feel that in comparison we are
spiritual pygmies. And it is not just a classic case of low
self-image! As I reflect on the prayer life of Martin
Luther, the Bible study habits of John Wesley, the endur-
ance of John Bunyan, and the commitment to service of
David Brainerd, I must confess my relative spiritual
immaturity. Few modern men could be classified with
those giants in their walk with the Lord.

One is led to ask how they did so well spiritually without the benefit of self-love teaching, if it is so important an
aspect of the Christian life. The converse is worth asking.
Why do we not far surpass them now, having the advantage of it? These are disturbing queries that put self-love
teaching in a questionable light. The testimony of the literature, hymnody, and biography of historical Christianity
causes us to ask, "Where has been the needed emphasis on
the love of self? How great can that need be today?"

SOURCE OF THE CONCEPT

Another factor that puts self-love theory in a doubtful
light is its source. We have already noted that self-love
apparently does not flow to us through the stream of
church history but, as we shall see, has been borrowed
from the more dubious waters of secular psychology. Of
course that is not *ipso facto* proof that it is unbiblical. We
recognized earlier the principle that all truth is God's
truth, but can we always put theories of secular psychology in the "truth" category? Frequently the answer is no.
The fact is, most major branches of secular psychology
have unbiblical presuppositions at their roots. Behaviorism sees man as a machine; psychoanalysis sees him
as a helpless victim of his unconscious; and humanistic
psychology views man as being by nature basically good.
(Those schools of psychology will be dealt with later.)
From those corrupt springs flow waters that are suspect

at best. Can we be sure that evangelical self-love theorists have boiled them sufficiently to remove all the contamination? The need for a very careful examination should be quite evident.

SELF-LOVE AS A SUBSTITUTE

Another reason to question current teaching on self-love is that it has become a substitute. In what ways? As we look at the claims made for self-esteem and the problems that are predicted for those who lack it, we realize that self-love has in many cases taken the place previously occupied by teaching on the victorious Christian life or sanctification. Ten years ago when a person came to his pastor with a sin problem, the pastor probably would have opened the Word of God and shared the liberating truth of the power available to the believer through the Holy Spirit to live in victory.

Today there is a good possibility that the pastor would remind him of his need to accept himself. The reason is that both of those approaches work in the same area. They make similar claims. Recall the list of social problems that are said to result from low self-esteem. It included such items as hatred, alcoholism, drug abuse, and violence. Rather than viewing those things as sins that have as their solution the cleansing power of the blood of Christ, they are seen as the consequences of low self-esteem and have as their solution the boosting of feelings of self-worth.

Could it be that evangelical self-love theorists simply are teaching the same biblical truth in psychological rather than in theological language? Of course that is possible, but the idea still calls for careful examination. Even if that proves to be true, a valid question is, Why not use biblical terms? Is it not confusing to switch from one system to another? Could not inaccuracy result? If we speak of sin as a result of human depravity rather than of low self-esteem, then our description connotes human responsibility. It also calls for a spiritual solution.

Regardless of what we do with the questions that arise
from this shift from a theological to a psychological perspective on the Christian life, it is obvious that the
psychological teaching on self-love has replaced what used
to be theological territory. Before we accept it as any sort
of substitute, we need to examine it carefully.

Our major concern, of course, is what the Bible teaches
on the subject. At this point we offer what may be to most
contemporary Christians a startling observation, namely,
that love of self is not taught explicitly anywhere in Scripture. That is interesting in light of the profound spiritual
implications drawn from the concept by its evangelical
proponents. How could it be that a matter so vital to
Christian living finds no development in the teaching of
Scripture? Some may answer that self-love is inherent in
the command to love our neighbor as ourselves (Matthew
22:39). Trobisch comments, "The command to love your
neighbor is never given without the command to love
yourself."[9] But the command to love yourself is never
given in Scripture. The idea may be *implied* in the
neighbor passage, but to say that it is given as a command
is reading into the words of our Lord. This passage and
others will be discussed in-depth in chapter 4. Suffice it
here to say that the Bible's silence should give us special
cause for reluctance to accept evangelical self-love theories without careful scrutiny.

LACK OF BIBLICAL CRITICISM

The sudden, extensive, and profound acceptance of self-
love by evangelicals gives rise to a final concern, related
to the first. That is the lack of critical biblical examination
of the subject. Most of what has been published has been by
proponents of self-love theory, and little of that has been

9. Trobisch, p. 11.

generated from a theological point of view. However, there are some notable exceptions. Two articles in *Christianity Today* (already cited) by John Piper and John R. W. Stott contain excellent critiques of the issue. In addition, Jay Adams, in his *Christian Counselor's Manual* (Nutley, N.J.: Presbyterian and Reformed, 1976), devotes about ten pages to an examination of self-love. These are fine pieces of work that raise penetrating questions. They are limited, however, by their length. A more comprehensive treatment is needed. This book is an effort to help meet that need. If it contributes to the serious study of this topic, that part of its purpose will be well served.

But there is a further motivation behind this book. It is always easier to wound than it is to heal, so the question comes, if not self-love, then *what?* A common concern expressed is, "If I shouldn't love myself, does that mean I should hate myself?" One of the positive results of the current evangelical interest in self-love may be the search for a solidly biblical alternative and its use in counseling. Although the critique of the theory occupies our primary attention in this volume, an alternative is proposed in the latter chapters.

2

Setting the Stage

In any play or film one of the most crucial factors is the setting or backdrop of the story. Imagine trying to watch a western that was filmed in Times Square or a tropical island scene shot in Alaska! It would be confusing to say the least, and perhaps even upsetting, as your mind tried desperately to put it all together.

To understand anything accurately the setting is of vital importance, because life is never lived in a vacuum; it is never played out on an empty stage. There is always a cultural structure of some kind influencing it.

The areas in which we will be working—philosophy, psychology, and theology—are no exception. As we try to understand the contemporary self-love revolution in evangelical Christianity it is essential that we explore the philosophical, psychological, and theological mood that has provided the setting for this phenomenon. Needless to say, in one chapter we cannot expect to be exhaustive, but we can get a feel for the current situation that will be of real help in understanding what is to follow.

Beginning with the philosophical context in which we live, we must first recognize the process involved in establishing a philosophy of life. Its beginnings are usually traced to the academic world, where new ideas are developed, perhaps as a reaction to the current philosophical scene, a new scientific development, a world war, or some other event. That new philosophy is then passed on to the public via the classroom, books, and other media. Still, the average person has not yet felt its impact. That is accomplished when the student or the reader begins to interpret the philosophy in everyday terms.

For example, the philosophy may have implications for education, so an educator develops a new curriculum or a new approach to teaching on that basis. The new idea may even be reflected in things such as clothing and hairstyle. Popular music, advertisements, and other areas of life may also communicate the new philosophy until ultimately its essence is picked up by the man on the street, who is often unaware that he is reflecting it or that he has changed. Yet that process of infiltration can reach to the deepest levels of life and influence our attitudes, our complete world view. For our purposes, we are not so much interested in the formal statement of the philosophies prevalent today as we are in the popular *versions* of those philosophies that our society has adopted. That is the aspect that has the most direct impact on our lives and thinking.

THE RISE OF EVOLUTIONARY THOUGHT

Apart from Christianity, the system that probably has had the greatest impact on western culture is modern science. It was born out of the work of Francis Bacon and his assertion that truth could be discovered through the inductive method. By induction Bacon thought that the "New Atlantis," his Utopia, would be created. Though his dream has hardly been achieved, science has given us a staggering number of accomplishments. But with science has also come the evolutionary hypothesis. On its publication in 1859, Charles Darwin's *Origin of Species* received an enthusiastic reception and became truth for many almost overnight. The reason for that immediate acceptance is that a crystallization of the evolutionary hypothesis was long awaited. Since the Renaissance, secular Western society had decided that it could do quite well without God. But there was one catch. Apart from God, the intellectuals had no explanation for origins. So they retained God in an awkward arrangement known as Deism. That belief, that God created the universe and then departed, leaving man to his own devices, kept God around as long as He was needed, but set Him aside so that He would not interfere with the progress that man was bringing to Western culture.

No doubt this was an uncomfortable state of affairs for the humanistic minds of secular culture, which found the need to give God any place somewhat embarrassing. The evolutionary hypothesis provided the long-awaited out. It was what Western man wanted to hear. Its significance resided in the conclusion that God now was not needed at all. Secular society could finally be rid of Him completely. The evolutionary pyramid put the amoebas and protozoans at the bottom and man at the top. He was now the most advanced and most important being in the universe. He had finally achieved the goal set by his ancient enemy in the Garden of Eden, "You will be like God" (Genesis 3:5).

Probably the first reaction to the exaltation of man through the evolutionary hypothesis was much like that of children who have been left alone at home for the first time. They have their universe all to themselves, but it is not long before the loss of the structure and security that Mom and Dad provided begins to be felt. So it was with man alone in the universe. He had finally come of age, only to find that he still was not big enough to control his world. Though mankind was now god, according to the evolutionary hypothesis, performing the functions of a god was a different thing.

Another disturbing shortcoming man encountered was that, though according to this system he now was god, he was also only an animal. Evolution, though distinguishing man *quantitatively* from other animals, did not do so *qualitatively*. That arrangement left man with some far-reaching problems. According to science, an animal is only a biological machine, and now man was in the same category. He had been stripped of his dignity. He was only an advanced machine.

Therefore, though man became a god, he lost on two counts. First, looking upward, he had no one to reach up to in time of trouble. Mom and Dad had left home for good, and now the kids were feeling the full impact. Also, looking inward, he had lost his human distinctiveness and had become merely an animal. That lowered his value and stole much of the meaning from life. Life was a collection of molecules—no more.

But this situation had one major plus for modern man; namely, that he was no longer accountable to a higher authority. When Mom and Dad leave the children at home there is always that "And when we get home . . ." element that has a sobering effect on the situation. But what if they were not coming back? No accountability! So the evolutionist had no God and no concern with judgment from above.

In addition, there is no basis for judgment by society. Man as an animal, a machine, cannot be blamed for his choices, for there is no external standard of judgment. He has moved beyond, or rather beneath, freedom and dignity. Therefore, the only valid conclusion that can be drawn from an evolutionary system is that man cannot be held morally responsible for his actions. The price man paid to enjoy this freedom from accountability and responsibility was the loss of God and His provision of structure and security, and the loss of personal meaning.

This human predicament is not felt so keenly in times of peace and prosperity, but war is another matter. In those times man recognizes most acutely his need for an assur-

ance that Someone has built purpose into life, and that He
has concern for him as an individual. So World Wars I and
II provided great problems for the evolutionists. The
theory of evolution is optimistic in nature. It speaks of
growth and progress—man is ever developing. He is even
learning by his mistakes. Science will solve the problems
of want and illness, and psychology and sociology will care
for man's internal and external behavioral problems.
Francis Bacon's "New Atlantis" was only a matter of time.
Even World War I was a step forward because it was so
horrible that from it man learned that he must settle his
differences using other means. Then came World War II
and the atomic bomb, and with it the shattering of the
evolutionary dream.

THE SHIFT TO EXISTENTIALISM

At that point, modern man was faced with a problem.
He had no God to call on, he himself was reduced to an
animal, and the theory did not seem to be working. And to
make matters worse, the options seemed quite limited.
The learning of the Renaissance and the Enlightenment
had brought him to this point. He had intellectually
burned his bridges to God; the theology of the Reforma-
tion was now unacceptable. Rudolf Bultmann expressed
clearly this attitude:

> *Man's knowledge and mastery of the world* have ad-
> vanced to such an extent through science and technology
> that it is no longer possible for anyone seriously to hold the
> New Testament view of the world—in fact, there is no one
> who does. What meaning, for instance, can we attach to
> such phrases in the creed as "descended into hell" or "as-
> cended into heaven"? We no longer believe in the three-
> storied universe which the creed takes for granted."[1]

1. Rudolf Bultmann, *Kerygma and Myth* (New York: Harper & Row,
   1961), p. 4.

A return to the authority of the Scriptures was simply not an option.

Modern man's dilemma then was this—he needed value as a person. Scientifically, he saw evolution as the only viable basis for his world view, but that stripped him of personal meaning and reduced him to an animal, a biological machine. Therefore, the only way to find personal fulfillment was to reject science, that is, science as he saw it—"naturalistic scientism"—for a nonscientific approach.

What was the significance of this rejection? It was a rejection of an objective approach to life; making decisions in terms of dollars and cents, future security, widely accepted medical findings, and so on. In a word, established probabilities were not to be used as a basis for getting the most out of life.

Rather, life was viewed subjectively—what gives me personal fulfillment, what speaks to me, what I enjoy, regardless of what science has calculated to be the probable consequences. This profound shift from the objective approach of science and its probabilities to a subjective basis for life is the essence of what is called "existentialism." Perhaps we should call this version "popular existentialism."

A formal definition of existentialism is not only beyond the scope of this book, but may be beyond the realm of possibility. Paul Vitz, in his excellent volume *Psychology as Religion: The Cult of Self-Worship*, suggests "Existentialism as a philosophy is notoriously hard to characterize rigorously." There are, however, some basic observations we can make regarding the nature of existentialism. Vitz notes, "The central concept is probably that of 'being there' (Dasein), by which is meant the intense fundamental awareness of one's experience."[2] We see here a strong

2. Paul Vitz, *Psychology as Religion: The Cult of Self Worship* (Grand Rapids: Eerdmans, 1977), p. 25.

self-orientation—an awareness of my being, my own existence.

In addition to self-awareness, there is the related issue of self-worth, self-importance, and personal rights—the right to *be*. Along with that self-awareness comes the responsibility of *becoming*, "the process of self-development or fulfilling one's potential."[3] An important distinction should be made here between naturalistic scientism with its evolutionary conclusions and existentialism. The former sees *humanity* as god, whereas the latter makes the *individual* a deity by placing "I" at the center of the universe. The advent of evolution produced an emphasis on mankind and the species. Here the focus is narrowed to the individual.

Though the interest taken in humanity by naturalistic scientism is erroneously based (human beings as the highest product of the evolutionary process), that approach is seen to be morally superior to existentialism. At least it gives one a philosophical basis for concern for his neighbor, since the latter is also a part of the highest species. But the existentialist places self first, and if anything happens to spill over to another person that is all well and good, but that is not the existentialist's objective or primary concern. If benefit to neighbor occurs, it is an accident of the system.

Not only does existentialism differ from the evolutionary concept in that it narrows its focus from the benefit of humanity to the fulfillment of the individual, but the approach to finding that fulfillment is also different. As indicated above, instead of allowing science to show the way to successful living, the existentialist follows the path of personal, subjective choice. Alasdair MacIntyre's definition of existentialism states that for the existential man, "rational first principles have been replaced by criterionless choices. Neither God nor nature is at hand to render

3. Ibid.

the universe rational or meaningful, and there is no background of socially established and recognized criteria in either knowledge or morals."[4]

Vitz recognizes the inconsistency of speaking of a criterionless choice and the impossibility of the application of this principle. He sees the bankruptcy of this approach reflected in Camus's conclusion that the only significant philosophical question is whether or not to commit suicide.[5] Though the average existentialist does not follow the principle of criterionless choice to its logical conclusion in his quest for self-fulfillment, *this tenet does free him to seek self-fulfillment in any way he sees fit.* That is significant. Many a parent about to perform the traditional disciplinary ritual has announced, "This is in your best interest." No doubt in most cases the discipline genuinely is designed for the child's good. It is quite another thing, however, for the *child* to determine the means to that same good. Assuredly that would result in a change in the procedure!

That is the case with the existential man. Under naturalistic scientism, the scientific establishment decided what was good for man and society. But the existentialist not only limits his primary concern to his own interests, he claims the right to define fulfillment and to achieve it in any way he chooses. We saw that in the rebellion of the antiwar movement of the '60s against the establishment, whether government or college administration. It was their assertion of their right to self-fulfillment and their right to pursue that fulfillment free from the dictates of "science."

Popular existentialism also deals with the nature of fulfillment. Existentialists' rejection of science is based on the denial that any system can effectively explain the universe. Modern science was the best man could do, and it

4. Ibid., p. 52.
5. Ibid., p. 53.

failed him. Since meaning could not be established by objective criteria, an attempt was made to find it subjectively. That rejection resulted in confidence only in the immediate and the direct. To believe in tomorrow required belief in a system; to believe in a process—for example, that hard work pays off—required acceptance of a system of thought. The only sort of self-fulfillment that did not demand confidence in a system was immediate sensual gratification. In fact, it may be said that the bottom line of existentialism is philosophical selfishness. People have always been selfish, but existentialism provided a philosophical justification for it. Self-gratification had now gained philosophical prestige.

Though the professional exponents of existentialism may not espouse all that has been written above, we believe that this is a fair representation of what existentialism is saying to the cross-section of those under its influence. It should be added that that includes all of us to one degree or another. The extent to which the tenets of existentialism have infiltrated the thinking of our society is immeasurable. Though it is not always seen in the blatant form described here, the attitudes and values of our society have been substantially affected in this direction.

There is no question that existentialism holds some pluses and minuses for secular man. On the plus side, existentialism allows him to retain his "deity" as the center of his personal universe. As such, he has not only the right, but also the responsibility to fulfill himself, and to do that in the way he prefers. He is no longer a biological machine manipulated by heredity and environment, but a person with freedom of choice and absolute value, at least in his own eyes.

But this system (or nonsystem) also has some negatives. The great problem with existentialism is that it does not work. It cannot, because there is only sufficient room for one god in any given universe. If my quest for fulfillment interferes with yours, something has to give. If you find fulfillment in punching people in the nose, you may have difficulty finding someone who is fulfilled by being punched! Your "thing" may be lounging at the beach, but the rest of the world probably will not organize to support your habit. This approach to life can only endure, even partially, in an affluent and generous society that will put up with and support a limited version of the "do your own thing" approach to life on a temporary basis. It would be impossible for anyone to follow existentialism to its logical . conclusion because ultimately fulfillment involves other people, and as soon as a man meets another person he has come face-to-face with another existential god.

EXISTENTIALISM'S RESULTS

EFFECTS ON THE INDIVIDUAL

What is modern man's solution to the limits of existentialism? He has developed a schizophrenic world view. He enjoys his individual existential deity as long as he can, but when forced to he reverts to the deification of naturalistic scientism with its requirement to live on an objective basis. In other words, for the most part modern man recognizes that to survive he must get up in the morning, go to work, and do what the boss tells him—all very nondivine and nonexistential from his perspective. That is "scientific" living. But in his personal life the story is different. Whenever he can and to whatever extent he can, modern man assumes the existential approach to life, seeing himself as the center of the universe and doing whatever pleases him. This explains in part the rise in divorce, alcoholism, drug abuse, and other problems. Its influence is also seen in the "rights" movements of today— women's rights, children's rights, right to a minimum income, and so on. That is why the rights of the mother and not her unborn baby are considered in abortion cases.

When she becomes the center of her universe, everything else must be judged accordingly. The problem of people's being used as "sex objects," is because the only *person* in the world is *me*. So we find people thinking "scientifically" one moment and "existentially" the next.

EFFECTS ON SOCIETY

The schizophrenic existence of modern man, who chooses to be existential when he can be and scientific when he must be, has had disastrous implications for society. Existentially man asserts, "I have a right to do what I please," but when it comes time to pay the consequences he reverts to his "naturalistic scientism" and pleads, "But I am not responsible for my actions. I am only a biological machine programmed by society." Thus we have no correlation between rights and responsibilities. There are manifold instances of this approach to life in our society, from trends in our judicial system to certain welfare programs, theories of child-rearing, and approaches to management. Needless to say, our society cannot long endure on this basis. The established principle that responsibility must be commensurate with authority cannot be ignored.

EFFECTS ON PSYCHOLOGY

Philosophical schizophrenia also reflects itself in psychology. The person who has had a minimum of exposure to psychology may have the impression that the discipline is composed of an essentially unified body of knowledge or a homogeneous theoretical structure. But that is not the case; psychology is deeply fragmented. What makes matters more confusing is that often a person being exposed to psychology is only introduced to one of its emphases almost to the total exclusion of the others. It is like the familiar illustration of the blind men describing an elephant. The one near the tail thinks the elephant is like a rope, the one touching a leg likens him to a tree trunk, and so on. So it is with psychology—some see the psychologist in a laboratory, others in a counseling room with a couch. Both are right, and there is more besides. The philosophical duality of our society has laid the groundwork for this fragmentation.

Behaviorism. That aspect of psychology called *behaviorism* is committed to treating psychology strictly as a "science." That is reflected in the name itself, which signifies that its scope is limited to those phenomena which can be observed and measured, namely behavior. Such intangible entities as soul or will are not explored. But behaviorist theory goes deeper than the mere exclusion of the soul or will. The strong evolutionary bias of behaviorism leads to the conclusion that those nonobservable factors do not exist at all. Thus the mechanistic model of man previously described under naturalistic scientism is not only adopted by behaviorism, but was also, at least in part, created by it. Because the evolutionary hypothesis views man as an animal, behaviorism makes no qualitative distinction between the two. Therefore behaviorism does extensive work in animal psychology in its efforts to study and understand man.

Behaviorism views man ostensibly as a complex computer that has been programmed by society. Man is seen to function on a stimulus-response basis; that is, a given stimulus produces a given response depending on how the person is programmed. There is no personal decision involved in the process. Therefore, behaviorism reduces man to a machine. The founder of behaviorism is usually considered to be John Watson, and its best known contemporary representative is B. F. Skinner.

Freudian psychology. A second major branch of psychology, Freudian psychology, has little to do with either of the philosophical trends we have mentioned. Though Freud was an evolutionist, that concept is not at the heart of his theoretical structure. Freud may be viewed as a pragmatist of sorts. Rather than following any preconceived philosophical bent, he developed his theory primarily by long hours of counseling, observing, and hypothesizing. At the beginning of his counseling career he used hypnotism to probe more deeply into his patients' personalities. That was soon exchanged for free association and dream analysis. It should be noted here that Freud developed his theory of personality through his study of some members of the most troubled segment of society. His conclusions regarding mankind were quite negative, and some have charged that that is a result of the specimens he chose to study. Freud viewed man as being prey to disturbances resulting from inadequate (or overadequate) passage through psychosexual stages prior to the age of five. Those disturbances are lodged in the unconscious mind where man cannot deal with them rationally. Thus man is a helpless victim of his unconscious.

Neo-Freudian psychology. Freud's successors, often labeled neo-Freudian psychologists, differed quite markedly from Freud at this point. Those psychologists served as something of a bridge that crossed from Freud, with his negative view of humanity, to humanistic psychology, a movement inspired by men such as Abraham Maslow and Carl Rogers. Actually, the neo-Freudian sector was quite humanistic in its own right, viewing man in a positive light (although the later writings of Erich Fromm, who is classified as a neo-Freudian, did stress the evil of man more clearly).

As the neo-Freudian movement developed into humanistic psychology, one of the forces that became a guiding light was existentialism. The writers of the neo-Freudian and humanistic groups give man credit for greater things than did Freud. That exaltation of man is not born of "science," since that has made him a mere machine. It is rather a blind faith, an optimism without a data base. It is like the existential leap in the dark. Some of the

psychologists in this neo-Freudian/humanist movement
openly espouse an existential orientation, but others do
not. Vitz notes that Rogers, though never having direct
contact with existentialism, "has developed a therapy with
important existential aspects."[6]

It is that last group of psychologists, beginning with the
neo-Freudian theorists and moving on into humanistic
psychology, who have developed the contemporary approach to self-love. In future chapters we will look at some
of the major contributors of this sector of psychology.

6. Ibid., p. 26.

3

Drawing Necessary Distinctions

One of my former students is a very lovely young woman who is blind. Her blindness resulted from a slight error a nurse committed while caring for her at birth. "Slight!" you say. Yes, slight in a technical sense, but overwhelming in its implications for Jane.

In most, if not *all* areas of life small factors are significant. The engineer building the bridge must be certain that the concrete receives just the right mix. The surgeon obviously has little room for error. For the farmer, planting or harvesting at just the right time becomes a crucial issue. In all of these areas, accuracy and precision are a must.

That fact may seem to be self-evident, but there is a desperate need to reemphasize this vital principle in some other important areas of life. Perhaps you are thinking, "But we live in such a technological age. How can you say there is any neglect of accuracy? It almost seems that we are *too* preoccupied with a concern for detail and the minute aspects of life." That may be true, but the problem is that the recognition of the importance of precision is restricted to certain areas of life. To be more accurate, I should say that it has been excluded from others that are just as crucial. In technology we respect and demand accuracy. But when it comes to man and his outlook on life, a disturbing, casual, easy-going, do-what-you-please mentality pervades our culture.

THE NEED FOR ACCURACY

Because philosophy and theology fall into the latter category, the tendency has been to deal with them with a very slack hand. So often a handy cliché, a superficial argument, or a loose line of reasoning are considered sufficient defense for a given point. After all, this is just so much theory. The thing that really counts is real-life experience, not cold doctrine. That attitude reflects the inroads that existentialism has made on contemporary thinking, and unfortunately evangelicals have not been immune.

We dare not allow that line of thinking to obscure the fact that doctrine, whether perceived to be cold or otherwise, in the long run will determine the nature of experience. The young couple exulting in the fresh glow of romance may argue, "We don't need those cold principles that are supposed to make for a good marriage. We are in love, and love will take care of everything. It is the experience that counts, not the theory." Most thinking people would quickly affirm that a relationship approached on that basis is headed for troubled waters.

The existential influence in our society, with its deemphasis of the importance of accuracy in the personal and interpersonal aspects of life (especially in philosophy and theology), has evidenced itself in a number of ways. The evangelical books that have gained the greatest popularity are frequently those that are nontechnical in nature. Heart-to-heart rather than mind-to-mind is the keynote of the day. Our interest is not in what is precise but "what speaks to me."

But without accuracy we will have very little of substance. By a few seemingly small changes or omissions we can make the Bible (or philosophy) say almost anything we want. A theology built on that basis turns out to be very unstable, because it says nothing that cannot, with a little adjustment, be changed to say something else. We may be sure that orthodoxy was not built by such casual methodology. The major issue confronting the Council of Nicea in A.D. 325 turned on the inclusion or exclusion of one Greek letter in one word of church doctrine, and that an *iota*, the smallest letter in the Greek alphabet! But had that council not convened and established orthodox doctrine on the deity of Christ, we might all be Arians today.

What does all of that have to do with our present study? As we proceed we will find that some weighty issues rest on fine distinctions that may seem to be insignificant. But this is the stuff out of which theology is made. If God designed the natural world with such precision, would He do less in His eternal Word, which will remain after heaven and earth have passed away? If we demand precision of those who work in sensitive technological areas (our doctors or pharmacists, for example), should we set a lower standard for ourselves as we seek to understand truths pertaining to the soul and how those truths operate and interrelate in our lives?

A second helpful principle we need to keep in mind is that there is much of real value in the various fields of study. In chapter 1 we noted that the major branches of psychology are built on many unbiblical presuppositions. That does not mean that we cannot use any of their findings, but it does mean that we must scrutinize them carefully. Many discoveries of modern medicine and science have been a real blessing to us. We all appreciate modern medical remedies. Such advances have made life easier for everyone.

However, there are other conclusions the secular sciences have drawn that we do not find quite so helpful. The new math, as an educational breakthrough, does not seem to excite anyone these days, at least in a positive way.

Some of the permissive educational philosophies that seemed so revolutionary during the past decade are the reason that educators now refer to that era as "the bad period." Then there are the theory of evolution and a host of other ideas that as the product of secular thought have been looked on with disfavor by most Christians.

How do we pick and choose among the many findings? Let me suggest a standard for measurement. Those conclusions that are closest to the data, tested in the lab, or subjected to other research are the safest. The ones that can be verified experimentally are the most trustworthy. When people step back from the data and begin to theorize, the possibility of error increases drastically. The further the thinking process is from the data the more room there is for a person to work in his own prejudices and presuppositions. For example, a scientist can study the various strata in the Grand Canyon and record what kinds of fossils he finds in each layer. It is an entirely different matter for him to assume that the processes that formed those layers were the same as those at work today, and therefore to conclude that it took so many millions of years for it to happen. Obviously, this sort of process is hardly repeatable. So in his leap from the fossil data to a theory the scientist has room to insert his presupposition that because only natural forces are at work in the universe, everything must be explained in that light.

So in borrowing from the secular world we can be far more comfortable with data that can be verified. We must especially be cautious when it comes to broad theories that give the theorist room to speculate. All truth may be God's truth, but much secular thought does not qualify as truth.

Realizing the necessity for precise distinctions and for verifiable data, we are ready to ask the question, Precisely what is self-love or self-esteem? William James, a psychologist who did some foundational work in this area many years ago and whose writings are still considered a bench mark, predates the formulation of contemporary self-love theory. He made careful distinctions as he developed his thinking on self-love, distinctions that aid us greatly in evaluating the modern version of this concept.

THE TEACHING OF WILLIAM JAMES

In *Theories of Personality*, Calvin S. Hall and Gardner Lindzey make the following observation: "William James in his famous chapter on the self in *Principles of Psychology*, 1890, chapter 10, set the stage for contemporary theorizing and much of what is written today about the self and the ego derives directly or indirectly from James."[1] In the chapter cited by Hall and Lindzey, a significant portion of what James has to say deals with self-love. There he touches on many issues that later became crucial in the development of self-theory. L. Edward Wells and Gerald Marwell observe, "William James is generally identified as the earlist self-psychologist and his writings are still standard reference for developmental discussions on self-esteem. James' early discussion is still considered definitive."[2]

Though from an earlier day, James was one of the most careful and systematic thinkers on the subject of self-love. Some of the fine distinctions he insisted on are largely ignored in the more speculative contemporary theories. For many of his findings James used his own self-awareness as his laboratory. Because of that we can easily verify much of what James is saying merely by looking within ourselves. It should be noted that here he is not making broad, speculative statements, but rather is attempting to

1. Calvin S. Hall and Gardner Lindzey, *Theories of Personality* (New York: John Wiley & Sons, 1970), p. 515.
2. L. Edward Wells and Gerald Marwell, *Self-Esteem: Its Conceptualization and Measurement* (Beverly Hills, Calif.: Stage Productions, 1976), p. 14.

categorize carefully the data derived from his subject. For that reason we can consider James's pronouncements in this area as trustworthy.

James's basic statement on the self is found in his *Psychology: Briefer Course*. He stated:

> Whatever I may be thinking of, I am always at the same time more or less aware of *myself*, of my *personal existence*. At the same time it is *I* who am aware; so that the total self of me, being as it were duplex, partly known and partly knower, partly object and partly subject, must have two aspects discriminated in it, of which for shortness we may call one the *Me* and the other the *I*.[3]

In recognizing that a person can be both the knower and that which is known, James was calling our attention to the fact that one of the distinct capabilities of a human being is his ability to have a relationship with himself. Not only do we relate to others and to the world around us, but we have the peculiar capacity to look inward and say, "I am a person. I have this or that ability. I am either happy or unhappy with what I see. I will do something to preserve or enhance my well-being."

James's work on this matter simply involved categorizing the various aspects of the I/Me relationship. In what ways do I relate to myself as a person? In seeking to answer that question James developed three categories. He called them self-feelings, self-love, and self-estimation. James observed that self-feelings are either positive or negative; that is, a person can feel either good or bad about himself. One of the synonyms that James used for positive self-feelings is self-esteem, a term that has been used widely in contemporary secular and evangelical self-love theory.

James cited several factors that influence a person toward either positive or negative self-feelings. The first is

3. William James, *Psychology: Briefer Course* (New York: Henry Holt, 1892), p. 176.

our nature, the basic personality orientation with which
we were born. He wrote, "These two opposite classes of
affection seem to be direct and elementary endowments of
our nature." He went on to say that often those feelings
do not appear to be rooted in objective reality:

> There is a certain average tone of self-feeling which each
> one of us carries about with him, and which is independent
> of the objective reasons we may have for satisfaction or
> discontent. That is, a very meanly conditioned man may
> abound in unfaltering conceit, and one whose success in life
> is secure, and who is esteemed by all, may remain diffident
> of his own powers to the end.[4]

In addition to seeing natural inclinations as a source of
self-esteem, James also postulated that performance is a
factor in inducing within us either positive or negative
self-feelings. Therefore, although a person is born with a
positive or negative orientation toward himself, his successes and failures in life will also influence those feelings.
One may be born with a positive self-orientation, but
through a series of failures that self-orientation may de-
cline; whereas a person born with a negative inclination
toward himself may, through a series of successes, become
much more positive in his self-attitude. Of the two (nature
and performance) James felt that performance was the
more influential. He believed that the "normal *provocative*
of self-feeling is one's actual success or failure, and the
good or bad actual position one holds in the world."[5]

James termed his second category of self-orientation
"self-love." He developed this concept under the heading
of "self-seeking" or "self-preservation." This self-love or
self-preservation relates primarily to action rather than
feeling. In making a distinction between self-feelings and
self-love James observed, " 'Self-love' more properly belongs under . . . acts, since what men mean by the name is

4. Ibid., p. 182.
5. Ibid.

rather a set of motor tendencies than a kind of feeling properly so called."[6] Elsewhere he stated, "What my comrades call my bodily selfishness or self-love, is nothing but the sum of all the outer acts which this interest in my body spontaneously draws from me."[7]

So James described self-esteem as a *feeling* and self-love as an *action*. Although his distinction here seems to be quite obvious, it is one that is often overlooked. The word *love* covers quite a broad spectrum. Therefore, in formulating a self-love theory there is a need to categorize the various applications of the term *love* to human existence and to designate the one that is in view.

James's concept of self-love refers to those things that a person does because by nature he is motivated to seek his best interests; when an individual feels hungry, he is motivated to eat; when tired, he seeks to find rest, and so forth. James has defined self-love with the primary focus on those actions that are necessary to care for ourselves and preserve our lives. Unfortunately, his careful differentiation between self-feelings (or self-esteem) and self-oriented acts (his self-love) is not made in many contemporary self-love theories. The implications of that failure will be seen later. Because self-love is an action word, it is also volitional in nature, since the decision to act must precede the act itself. Thus self-love involves the will—a person must decide to care for himself.

James described a third type of self-orientation that he called "cold intellectual self-estimation." In other words, the individual has the ability to take an objective inventory of himself and his capacities. James supports the existence of this capability in man by noting:

No matter how he *feels* about himself, unduly elated or unduly depressed, he may still *know* his own worth by

6. Ibid.
7. William James, *The Principles of Psychology*, 3 vols. (New York: Henry Holt, 1890), 1:320.

measuring it by the outward standard he applies to other men and counteract the injustice of the feeling he cannot wholly escape. This self-measuring process has nothing to do with the instinctive self-regard we have hitherto been dealing with.[8]

So of the three relationships a person can have with himself, we see that self-feeling is emotional in nature; self-love focuses on will and action; and self-estimation involves the intellect. Though James never described his categories in those terms, he discerned the fact that as individuals we can relate to ourselves through our emotions, will, and intellect, the three elements that constitute personhood.

The three categories also operate somewhat independently of one another. You can objectively see yourself as a success but still have negative self-feelings. You can decide to care for yourself even though you may have negative self-feelings. Even though I may be suffering from a low self-image, I probably will still arrange for my next meal, provide clothing for myself, and find housing. So what James calls self-feeling is a separate category from the one he designated as self-love.

Which of the three categories corresponds most closely to the contemporary concept of self-love? The term itself does not give us the answer, since "love" can have a multitude of meanings; a physical relationship, a sentimental attachment, an act that is beneficial to another, or a host of other things. Therefore we must see how the term *love* is being used.

Today's self-love is essentially emotional in its make-up. It involves liking oneself or feeling positive about oneself. So it seems that the contemporary idea fits squarely into James's emotion-oriented category of "self-feeling," rather than to those actions of self-preservation that James labeled "self-love."

8. Ibid., p. 328.

It should be clear that we are speaking about two different phenomena, two different types of self-relationships. One focuses on emotions, the other on will and action. We have also seen that the word *love* covers them both. Because of that, unless we emphasize the distinction two people may be speaking of self-love (both using a correct term) but referring to two distinctly different concepts. That is why it is so important when we speak of self-love to ask ourselves which of those types of love is in view—feeling, or will and action? When James used the term *self-love* he had will and action in mind; the contemporary self-love theorists usually refer to feelings.

4

What Does Scripture Say?

Since the time of Sigmund Freud psychology has abounded in personality theories, patterns of ideas that seek to describe what personality is and what makes it work. Formulators such as Carl Jung, Alfred Adler, Karen Horney, Harry S. Sullivan and a host of others have contributed to this effort, each building on his or her predecessors but also breaking some new ground.

The greatest book ever written on personality, however, is the Bible. There we find concept after concept that speak of what man is like and how he does and *should* relate to others, including God, his friends, business associates, spouse, children, and himself. The Bible speaks of love and hate, pride and humility, joy and depression, moral victory and defeat. It speaks of the intellect, the emotions, and the will, and how they should interrelate. That list of the aspects of personality that the Bible discusses could be expanded, not to mention what it has to say about each of those areas.

The Silence of Scripture

In view of this biblical concern with personality, it might be assumed that if self-love were a significant aspect of personality the Word of God would have a great deal to say about it. This would be true especially if self-

49

love were crucial to a happy, productive life and wholesome relationships with ourselves and others. It is hard to imagine that a book that has so much to say about the human personality would have a blind spot in an area of such special importance.

The fact is, though, that the Bible contains no explicit, positive teachings about self-love as it is described by contemporary theorists. As we shall seek to demonstrate, there is no direct biblical exhortation or encouragement to the individual to have positive self-feelings. Nor are any of the popular terms such as "feel good about yourself" or "like yourself" used. The absence of scriptural teaching at this point certainly is notable. If we believe that the Bible is the sufficient guide for the church, can it be that here is an issue pertinent to joyful and victorious living that the Bible fails to discuss?

Now we must recognize that some things are outside the range of subjects discussed by Scripture. Biblical pronouncements made in any area are true, but it is obvious that the Bible is not an encyclopedia. Certain topics are excluded, but the biblical silence does not mean they are condoned or condemned. Some want to argue that self-love is part of that "things not discussed" list, but that raises a problem. As stressed by its own advocates, self-love would lie too close to the heart of Scripture to be considered irrelevant to its message or unrelated to its concerns. It seems fair to say that if the evangelical theory of self-love is valid, the Scriptures should expound it thoroughly. The fact that they do not must be faced.

But this fact has not been faced. Seldom if ever in the voluminous writings on the subject do we find a recognition of the absence of explicit teaching on self-love in the Bible. Few serious attempts have been made to account for that silence. At this point it is fair to ask, "But doesn't the Bible teach that I should love my neighbor as myself? So if I am going to love my neighbor, I must love myself first." It is interesting to note that the first contemporary self-love advocate to use this passage as biblical support for self-love was not an evangelical but Erich Fromm, a psychologist and thoroughgoing, self-declared humanist.

The mandate to love our neighbor as ourselves is found in a number of passages of Scripture, in both the Old and New Testaments. When asked, "Teacher, which is the great commandment in the law?" (Matthew 22:36), Jesus responded by citing two commandments. The first requires wholehearted love toward God (vv. 37-38), and the second commands love toward our neighbor (v. 39). Christ concluded by noting that "On these two commandments depend the whole Law and the Prophets" (v. 40).

This command to love our neighbor as ourselves is seen by many not only as biblical justification, but a biblical mandate to love ourselves. Jay Adams effectively counters this idea.

> When Christ said that the whole law could be summed up in *two* commandments (love for God and love for one's neighbor), He intended to say exactly that and nothing else. Yet some Christians (with a psychologizing bent) and some psychiatrists who are Christians are not satisfied with that; they (dangerously) add a third commandment: love yourself.
>
> . . . the fact that Christ distinguished but *"two* commandments" (vs. 40) is decisive. Had He intended to stress a third (particularly when one of the other two was dependent upon it) He could not have done so by using the language He employs in this passage. Such psychologizing of the passage erases its plain intent and seriously diverts its stress. . . . It is incorrect and dangerous, therefore, to make a large point out of that about which Christ did not make a point at all (and, indeed, which He explicitly excluded by the limiting word *two*).[1]

1. Jay E. Adams, *Christian Counselor's Manual* (Nutley, N.J.: Presbyterian and Reformed, 1976), pp. 142-43.

Adam's argument is difficult to answer and, to our knowledge, has not been answered by self-love proponents. If Christ had wanted to command people to love themselves a third clear directive would seem to be needful, especially if a lack of self-love is the problem of epidemic proportions and far-reaching consequences that we are told it is.

The reason Christ did not give a third command could be that the type of self-love about which He was speaking was assumed to be something people already possessed. It must be something we do automatically, instinctively. There was no need to command that kind of self-love. Paul also attests to the universality of that kind of self-love when he asserts that a husband should love his wife as he loves his own flesh (Ephesians 5:28-29). The assumption of self-love or self-preservation clearly is present. In fact, in both passages the argument rests on it. All people are assumed to love themselves in some sense. The obvious message is, "*Since* you love yourself, do likewise to your neighbor or your wife."

The universality of self-love taken for granted by these passages presents a major problem for contemporary self-love theory. One of its foundational presuppositions is that many people are plagued by a lack of self-love. Our society is said to be suffering greatly from this malady. If the Bible is in fact speaking of the same kind of self-love that modern theory prescribes, then psychologists must be mistaken about the epidemic lack of self-love.

Though usually passed over by many self-love adherents, this difficulty is recognized by Trobisch, who seeks to explain the situation:

> The question now is how Jesus could assume that in his listeners this self-love . . . is naturally present. Part of the answer may lie in the fact that the people of Jesus' time were more composed and less neurotic than modern man. They found it easier to acquire self-acceptance and to like

themselves. Therefore, Jesus could assume that his hearers had learned to accept themselves to a degree people today have yet to learn. What was presumed as a natural characteristic in their time is something which is difficult for modern man to acquire.[2]

As an attempt to reconcile the "neighbor" passage with self-theory, this explanation is difficult to accept on several counts. The first is that human nature is not as fluid as Trobisch represents it. To say that there is a minor relative difference in human nature from era to era might be permissible. However, to argue that self-acceptance was the assumed norm in Christ's day while today its absence is epidemic strains our understanding of human personality.

Second, even if people accepted themselves in Christ's day that self-acceptance certainly did not do for them what self-love proponents claim it will do. A brief look at life in those times, including some of the lists of behavioral problems given by Paul (see Ephesians 4:17-19), reveals a less-than-ideal portrait of humanity.

Third, based on the language used, it is difficult to accept the thesis that Christ and Paul were speaking of some sort of transient self-love that has a tendency to disappear and then reappear in society. Consider Paul's assertion in Ephesians 5:29: "For no one ever hated his own flesh." That statement has the ring of a universal pronouncement true in all ages.

So the problems of using Matthew 22 or Ephesians 5 as a biblical basis for self-love are very real. Those passages indicate that some sort of self-love is a universal commodity—an inherent characteristic of humanity. The self-theorist using those verses would prove too much; he may win the battle but he would lose the war. He may demon-

2. Walter Trobisch, *Love Yourself* (Downers Grove: Inter-Varsity, 1976), p. 12.

strate that we should love ourselves, but at the same time
he would do away with the need for his theory.

How then should we understand what Jesus and Paul
are saying? It could be that they are referring to a type
of self-love *other than* that described in contemporary
evangelical literature. One argument for this conclusion is
that it squares with reality. We know that many people do
not have positive self-feelings—a good self-image. Such
self-feelings apparently are not an inherent part of human
nature, but we all have a bent toward self-preservation.

The Biblical Words for "Love"

Another reason for believing that the self-love spoken of
in Scripture is not the type advocated by contemporary
writers has to do with the biblical words for "love."

Surprisingly little attempt to derive an accurate biblical
definition of love is made in evangelical self-love literature. But care should be maintained to distinguish between the two basic Greek words that are translated
"love" in the New Testament. Those are the familiar word
agapē and its verb form *agapao*, and *philia* and its verb
form *phileō*. (In the case of those two terms, the noun
form is essentially the same in meaning as the verb;
therefore, we will use the noun primarily. No distinction
between the noun and verb is intended by this use of the
noun unless specifically stated.)

In our review of the self-love of psychology and
evangelicalism it has become evident that both advocate
the emotional, self-feeling variety. We are told to "like
ourselves," "feel good about ourselves," "be fond of ourselves," and so on. One writer plainly states, "Love itself
is an emotion."[3] Passages such as the following demonstrate that feelings are at the heart of the matter:

3. Maurice E. Wagner, *The Sensation of Being Somebody* (Grand
Rapids: Zondervan, 1975), p. 234.

Most of us have mixed feelings about ourselves. We fluctuate between periods of relative contentment and times of self-dissatisfaction. Sometimes we like ourselves; sometimes we don't. When we feel right about ourselves, we are happy, confident, relaxed, and alert. When we don't, we become pressured, anxious, irritable, or "down."[4]

Numerous other such statements could be cited that clearly describe self-love as being essentially emotional and thus corresponding to William James's "self-feelings." To which New Testament word for "love" do those self-feelings correspond?

Narramore is one of the few evangelical writers who gives attention to this matter of the New Testament words for love. He attempts a formal definition of love in *You're Someone Special.* His point is that the type of love termed "self-love" does not correspond with *philia,* but rather with the more prominent word *agapē. Philia,* Narramore says, "implies ardent affection or a love characterized by fiery impulse. . . ." *Agapē,* on the other hand, "has the flavor of esteem or regard." Narramore applies those terms by observing:

> *Agapē,* then, focuses on a person's value and significance. It is not an emotional, ecstatic adoration, nor is it the feeling we have when we "fall in love." It certainly is not an erotic feeling. Instead, agape love is a deep attitude of esteem and respect. This is the basic meaning of biblical self-love. It is a valuing or esteeming ourselves as significant individuals.[5]

For his definition Narramore draws from *Faussett's Bible Dictionary.* Although Faussett is a fine commentator, he is not at his best in analyzing the distinction between *philia* and *agapē.* Closer study reveals those conclusions to be inaccurate.

4. Bruce Narramore, *You're Someone Special* (Grand Rapids: Zondervan, 1978), p. 11.
5. Ibid., p. 38.

Philia generally refers to a natural human affection, fondness, or liking. Frederick Godet defines it as *"to cherish,* love in the sense of personal attachment,"[6] and B. F. Westcott as "the feeling of natural love."[7] R. C. H. Lenski agrees: *"Philia* expresses the love of mere personal affection or liking." He goes on to note that *philia* does not include the concept of "intelligence or high purpose."[8] The idea seems to be that the affection involved is not based primarily on calculated analysis of a situation and the people involved, nor is it basically volitional. It is a natural, uncalculated enjoyment of another person. The correspondence between the descriptions above and those used in self-love theory is striking.

As to the essential meaning of *agapē* in biblical literature, Ethelbert Stauffer states the matter succinctly by noting that it includes "the thoughts of selection, of willed address and readiness for action."[9] Thus he isolates the two basic elements of *agapē*—will and action. Those two elements have also been cited as primary ingredients in the definition of *agapē* by most scholars who have sought to do a comprehensive study of the word. Both terms may not always be used, because they are closely related on a functional basis, that is, volition produces action.

Stauffer believes that *agapē* gained its strength, which it lacked in classical literature, from its association with *aheb,* the Hebrew word for love used in the Old Testament passage from which Jesus quoted (Leviticus 19:18). Stauffer expresses the Old Testament meaning of *aheb* by

6. Frederick Louis Godet, *Commentary on the Gospel of John,* 2 vols. (Grand Rapids: Zondervan, 1969), 2:445.
7. Brooke Foss Westcott, *The Gospel According to St. John* (London: James Clarke, 1958), p. 302.
8. R. C. H. Lenski, *The Interpretation of St. John's Gospel* (Minneapolis: Augsburg, 1961), p. 1419.
9. Ethelbert Stauffer, "Love in Judaism," *Theological Dictionary of the New Testament,* ed. Gerhard Kittel, trans. Geoffrey W. Bromiley, 10 vols. (Grand Rapids: Eerdmans, 1965), 1:39.

noting, "The love of God for Israel (Dt. 7:13) is not impulse but will; the love for God and the neighbor demanded of the Israelite (Dt. 6:5; Lv. 19:18) is not intoxication but act."[10] Again volition and action are central. Showing the close relationship between the two words, Stauffer observes, "This word [*agapē*], which is widely used in the LXX [the Greek Old Testament], is in the overwhelming majority of cases a rendering of *aheb* and derivatives."[11]

The Old Testament understanding of volitional love is carried over into the gospels as expressed by *agapē*. "For Jesus, too, love is a matter of will and action."[12] So also is the *agapē*, the love of God in Pauline literature. "It is the orientation of the sovereign will of God to the world of men and the deliverance of this world."[13]

W. E. Vine defines *agapē* by asserting that "obviously this is not the love of complacency, or affection. . . . It was an exercise of the Divine will in deliberate choice."[14] The same idea is evident in man's love for God. "Christian love has God for its primary object, and expresses itself first of all in implicit obedience to His commandments."[15] Vine further delimits *agapē* by observing what it is not: "Christian love, whether exercised toward the brethren, or toward men generally is not an impulse from the feelings, it does not always run with the natural inclinations, nor does it spend itself only upon those for whom some affinity is discovered."[16]

Likewise, William Evans describes *agapē* as involving

10. Ibid., p. 38.
11. Ibid., p. 22.
12. Ibid., p. 48.
13. Ibid., p. 49.
14. W. E. Vine, *An Expository Dictionary of New Testament Words*, 3 vols. (Westwood, N. J.: Revell, 1966), 3:21.
15. Ibid., p. 16.
16. Ibid.

"a clear determination of will."[17] Lenski defines it as being "the love of intelligence, reason, and comprehension, coupled with corresponding purpose."[18] G. Abbott-Smith attributes to *agapē* "the spiritual affection which follows the direction of the will, and which, therefore, unlike that feeling which is instinctive and unreasoned, can be commanded as a duty."[19]

The definitions we have established for *agapē* and *philia*, if at all accurate, should be reflected in the way those terms are used in the New Testament. Some find that *agapē* is used frequently as a command, but *philia* never is, which is what we might expect based on the definitions given above. A command directed toward our will and action is appropriate, but a command to have warm feelings toward another *(philia)* appears to be contrary to our human capacities. That is true especially of the command to love strangers and our enemies. Many of those commands stipulate the *action* that is required: "Love [*agapate*] your enemies, and pray for those who persecute you" (Matthew 5:44).

But which of those words corresponds most closely to the love we find in self-love theory? It should be clear that it is *philia*, with its emphasis on affection, liking, attachment, a feeling of natural love, cherishing, and so on. Almost all of the terms used to define *philia* are found in the descriptions of self-love as taught by contemporary theorists. Carl Rogers, a psychologist, has been a leading light to many evangelical self-love advocates. As we shall see, they have borrowed heavily from his writings. It is instructive to note the close similarity between *philia* and

17. William Evans, "Love," in *International Standard Bible Encyclopaedia*, ed. James Orr, 5 vols. (Grand Rapids: Eerdmans, 1939), 3:1932.
18. Lenski, p. 1419.
19. G. Abbott-Smith, *A Manual Greek Lexicon of the New Testament*, (Edinburgh: T & T Clark, 1956), p. 3.

Rogers's definition of positive regard. He states, "In general, positive regard is defined as including such attitudes as warmth, liking, respect, sympathy, acceptance."[20] *Philia*-type qualities are also apparent in many evangelical writers: "All of us want to feel good about ourselves."[21] This is clearly not a statement of will and action but of feelings and attachment. The focus is on feelings, emotion, liking, and related ideas. In contrast, the biblical idea of *agapē* and William James's category of self-love basically are the same and are composed of will and action.

Returning to Matthew 22:39 we observe that *agapaō* is the word Jesus used. In view of the volitional and action connotation of *agapaō*, it is inappropriate to represent that verse as demanding the type of self-love advocated today. This conclusion is shared by Piper, who observes that the parallel teaching in Luke is illustrated by the story of the "good Samaritan" (Luke 10:25-37). He notes that in the narrative love is characterized by the willingness "to interrupt your schedule, and use up your oil, wine, and money to achieve what you think is best for your neighbor."[22] Action, not feeling, is in view.

This understanding of the "neighbor" passage also explains why Christ assumed this type of self-love to be universal. Self-preservation—the inclination to meet our own needs, to feed ourselves and find shelter—is part of our human make-up. Normally it takes no urging to motivate a person to care for himself. On the contrary, it usually requires restraint to stop such satisfaction of need. Jesus

20. C. R. Rogers, "A Theory of Therapy, Personality, and Interpersonal Relationship, as Developed in the Client-Centered Framework," in *Psychology: A Study of a Science*, ed. S. Koch, (New York: McGraw-Hill, 1959), vol. 3, *Formulations of the Person and the Social Context*, p. 208.
21. Bruce Narramore and Bill Counts, *Freedom from Guilt* (Irvine, Calif.: Harvest House, 1974), p. 8.
22. John Piper, "Is Self-Love Biblical?" *Christianity Today*, 12 August 1977, pp. 6-9.

says that a person should do likewise for his neighbor, and in other places, for a stranger or even an enemy. No one needs to *command* me to meet my own needs; that response is built in. But when it comes to meeting my neighbor's needs, I have not been wired by nature to be automatically sensitive to his concerns. So Christ's command calls me to that kind of awareness.

Paul's initial directive to the husband also reflects the *agapē* mood of Ephesians 5. "Husbands, love your wives, just as Christ also loved the church and gave Himself up for her" (v. 25). This passage is imperative in nature and calls for action, just as Christ did when He gave Himself. The term "cherish" (v. 29), at first glance, may seem to connote more of a feeling than an action, but the matter is clarified when we recognize that the basic meaning of this word is "to warm."[23] Therefore Paul's use of *agapaō* includes feeding and warming, the basic care of the body. The self-love of Ephesians 5:28-29 is that of self-preservation. Warm feelings are not at issue.

A Warning from Scripture

As demonstrated, the incompatibility of Matthew 22 and Ephesians 5 with modern self-love theory closes the door on the only biblical passages that could be interpreted as explicitly teaching self-love. Its proponents lay claim to no other explicit biblical teaching, nor is any other verse an obvious candidate. This silence casts doubt on the claim that the self-love of contemporary teaching is a biblical concept.

However, even more damaging is the correspondence of the love described by self-theory to *philia*. We should hasten to add that *philia* is a wonderful kind of love in itself. It speaks of those divine and human affections that supply so much joy to life. But what of *philia* affection for one-

23. Joseph Henry Thayer, *Greek-English Lexicon of the New Testament* (Grand Rapids: Zondervan, 1970), p. 282.

self, the kind of self-love described by contemporary writers? What does the Bible say of that? Second Timothy 3:1-4 makes a direct statement about this *philia* type of self-love: "But realize this, that in the last days difficult times will come. For men will be *lovers of self*, lovers of money, boastful, arrogant, revilers, disobedient to parents, ungrateful, unholy, unloving, irreconcilable, malicious gossips, without self-control, brutal, haters of good, treacherous, reckless, conceited, lovers of pleasure rather than lovers of God" (italics added).

The term Paul uses here for "lovers of self" is *philautos*, which is a compound of *philia* and *autos*, the Greek words for love and self (this is the only use of this term in the New Testament). The fact that the definition of *philia* matches so closely that of self-love as described today is substantial evidence that the passage is speaking of that kind of love.

Two factors should immediately command our attention in this text. The first is that its context is "the last days." How often we hear Christians say, "These must be the last days." Of course they are referring to that time characterized by the attitudes Paul describes so pointedly. Yet it seems that somehow many evangelicals have not joined together what is joined together here, namely that the last days and a sinful self-love will go together, and neither is to be applauded.

A second reason Paul's teaching should capture our attention is that today the teaching of self-love is not just an evangelical phenomenon. That should concern us because it serves to link self-love theory even more directly with 2 Timothy 3. If it *were* merely an evangelical doctrine, it would seem strange that Paul makes it a prominent feature of the last times, but since secular as well as evangelical thinking is saturated by the concept we must consider it a hallmark of the present day. John Piper aptly describes our times: "For a decade the cult of the self (to use Thomas Howard's phrase) has been expanding phenomenally fast and its professional members take every chance they get to put a mirror in front of us and tell us to like what we see."[24]

This is evidenced on a popular level with the advent of periodicals such as *Self* magazine and best sellers telling us we are "OK" and that we should "look out for number one." It would seem naive to conclude that this secular proliferation of the self-love theme and its evangelical development are unrelated. The *extent* of that relationship will be seen later, but the *fact* of it hardly can be denied.

For the most part 2 Timothy 3 has been ignored by the proponents of self-love. There has been little serious attempt to explain its apparent condemnation of the kind of self-feelings they advocate. That failure is quite outstanding and should cause us to proceed with extreme caution in that area.

24. Piper, p. 6.

5

The Basis for Self-Love

An obvious question suggests itself at this point. If the self-love of contemporary teaching is not derived from the explicit teaching of Scripture, on what do present-day evangelicals base the idea? Where do they turn for biblical support? A few have recognized the weakness of using Matthew 22:39 as a biblical basis and have looked elsewhere. Bruce Narramore is one who has verbalized this need:

> I remember the first time the idea of loving myself crossed my mind. I was talking with a group of friends and one of them stated, "Christ said that we were to 'love our neighbors as ourselves.' This," he continued, "obviously means that we should love ourselves. Why else would Christ say 'as yourself'?"
>
> Since that time, I have heard many other speakers offer this view. Each time, I have the same uneasy reaction. I believe these people are right when they tell us to love ourselves. But they are wrong in trying to base self-love on this passage.[1]

Evangelical writers such as Narramore who recognize that Jesus' command to "Love your neighbor as yourself" does not teach self-love still seek to prove that we have a

1. Bruce Narramore, *You're Someone Special* (Grand Rapids: Zondervan, 1978), pp. 21-22.

scriptural justification for doing so, even though the Bible does not affirm it in so many words. The argument is that biblical *reasons* for self-love are present; therefore, self-love is legitimate and necessary for the Christian if he is to be all that God wants him to be.

But this approach to the matter is weak at best. To illustrate, let us consider a similar approach to prayer. We may reason that since God is our heavenly Father we should bring our requests to Him as we do to our earthly fathers. Since He is all-knowing He will hear us when we pray. Because He is loving He will want to answer. As He is all-powerful He will be able to answer. Therefore, we conclude that prayer is a wonderful privilege of God's children.

Based on the apparent soundness of that theory, would it not be surprising if prayer were never mentioned in the Bible? What if it did not tell us about the prayers of others, did not teach us to pray and encourage us to do so? What if answers to prayer were not found in Scripture, or if the consequences of our failure to pray were not pressed upon us? Would not the absence of all that be very troublesome to us and cause us to reexamine our theory, although it may appear that the Scripture afforded us a basis for prayer? The point is that the theoretical bases and the application necessarily go together. The absence of the latter is good reason to doubt the soundness of the former.

So it is with self-love. Even though the theory may sound convincing, the absence of such clear teaching brings the matter of its scriptural basis into question. Before we examine the scriptural rationale used by evangelical self-love proponents, we must first take a closer look at the structure of self-love thinking. What precisely is the foundation stone of this popular theory?

Perhaps the simplest way to state it is this: "I am *lovable*, therefore I should love myself." It is important that we underscore this simple hypothesis, for in it lies the crux of self-theory as found in its most popular secular form and in virtually all of its evangelical formulation. It contains in seed form all of the major concepts that form the foundation of modern self-theory. At least five principles in particular are indispensable to this teaching and need to be examined.

The first three are implied in the statement, "I am lovable." This affirmation raises the question, who is the *I*? Who is permitted to make this statement? Is its application restricted to an elite group of people who are living on a certain spiritual plane or who have made some special contribution to society?

Unconditional Love

The answer of course is to the contrary. The *I* is all people at all times, regardless of how they are living, no matter what they are doing. Lovability is unaffected by who we are or what we do, whether right or wrong. The familiar term is *unconditional* love or acceptance. The individual is unconditionally lovable, and therefore should be unconditionally loved, respected, accepted, valued, or esteemed (all synonyms for essentially the same thing). This principle of unconditional acceptance is a basic, foundational principle of self-theory. If it were otherwise, if self-love were based on performance, then we would have to say to the individual, "I don't know if you really ought to love yourself. I would have a bad self-image too, if I were living the way you are. What you need to do is confess, repent, make amends to those whom you have hurt, and then you might have some reason to love yourself."

Such language is, of course, foreign to contemporary self-theory, both the secular and evangelical varieties. This is exactly what the counselor would *not* say to the individual. He would rather seek to demonstrate to him his lovability, that is, unconditional acceptability. We need to be clear that we are not just talking about accepting a person as he is when he comes in his contrition, his sorrow of heart for the past and his desire to change, to reach out for help to effect, that change. We are also talking about acceptance of the person who is bent on continuing in his sin without remorse. That is the implication implicit in the idea of unconditional love.

Based on Humanness

In a sense the term *unconditional love* makes no sense, because there must be some underlying basis for love. And there is in fact just such a basis in self-theory, the same one postulated both by secular and evangelical teachers, and that basis is *humanness*. A person is lovable simply because he *is* a human being, an individual. That is the second basic principle of modern self-theory.

This principle, from a logical perspective, is the safest basis for unconditional acceptance that can be found. If any other requirement were laid down I might not meet it, no matter how generous the criteria may be. But with this one I am safe. I still do not have to *do* anything; I only have to *be*. *Being* is enough; it qualifies everyone all of the time. Being is one thing I did not bring about. I had nothing to do with it. It has come to me without my active involvement. Therefore, by unconditional love we are speaking of love on the basis of being rather than doing.

One implication of this teaching is the place of grandeur that it gives to the human being. I am lovable just because I am human; therefore being human, in and of itself, regardless of what I do with my humanness, must have some sort of independent value or worth. It is by itself a sufficient claim to respect and esteem.

Unaffected by Performance

A third principle of contemporary self-theory that is also inherent in unconditional love is that our performance cannot affect our lovability. Regardless of how badly we feel or how cantankerous we may be, those actions cannot be detrimental to our basic acceptability.

This third principle has at least one connotation that is often overlooked. Self-love advocates usually think of performance in terms of the negative and rejoice that, despite our perverseness, we are still worth loving. But that concept also locks us into the conclusion that the *good* people do also has no positive effect on lovability. For example, a marriage partner may work, and sacrifice, and continually give of himself or herself to be the best mate possible. But according to the no-performance theory, that person should not be considered any more lovable (or more esteemed or respected) than the one who is unfaithful to the marriage, neglects the children, or whatever. The no-performance approach to life becomes extremely bland. If nothing I do will make any difference in my acceptability to you, why try? Why bother?

SELF-LOVE THE RESULT

Just as the last two principles above are a pair, one positive and the other negative, so too are the fourth and fifth propositions. We need to begin with a restatement of the basic assertion of self-theory: I am lovable, therefore I should love myself. We have been dealing primarily with the first half of that statement. Now we are ready to consider the full statement.

My lovability places on me the obligation to love myself. That is a duty, a necessity for happy and productive living, a prerequisite to relating well to others and contributing to society. To fail here is not only to rob myself but also to cheat others. Since a lack of proper self-love will hinder me from becoming the person I am designed to be, I will be unable to make my full contribution to those around me.

That line of reasoning could lead to a rather startling

conclusion; not to love myself is really a form of selfishness because in so doing I rob others of the benefits of my personal development!

SELF-LOVE NOT SELFISH

In fact, that conclusion is the heart of our last principle; self-love is not selfishness. If I can do my best for others by loving myself, then self-love is a very unselfish thing to do. Along with this it is asserted that self-love also is not pride. According to the theory, that is true first of all because we are in fact lovable; therefore self-love is merely a recognition of what we are. Second, we are told that the proud person really lacks genuine self-love and that his apparent pride is just a cover-up for his feelings of inferiority and inadequacy. That last point ought to be of special interest to evangelicals who traditionally have viewed self-love as selfishness and pride. We are being assured, however, by self-love proponents that such is not the case. Some even go so far as to say that self-love is an expression of humility.

So we have seen that self-love theory is based on a seemingly simple statement: "I am lovable; therefore I should love myself." The idea may seem to be sound biblically, but no Scripture can be produced to support it. On the contrary, as we consider some of its implications we cannot help but note its overwhelming compatibility with the teaching of existentialism as developed in chapter 2. The two are part of the same philosophical package. As a matter of fact, we might say that self-theory is merely the psychological expression of existentialism. The latter asserts that the individual is god. The self-theorist attributes to the individual the godlike quality of being intrinsically lovable. Likewise, existentialism upholds the right of the individual to do whatever he pleases. Self-theory grants him the right to be loved while he is doing it. This close link between existentialism and self-love theory is demonstrated effectively by Paul Vitz in his fine volume (see chapter 2).

It is apparent that self-theory even in its evangelical formulation did not receive its primary impetus from the Bible. For almost two thousand years theologians studied Scripture without discovering the doctrine of self-love as we now have it. However, a decade or so after its debut in psychology it appeared among us. It is no coincidence that there are many parallels between the secular and Christian theories. Often evangelical writers themselves will mention the teachings of Carl Rogers or some other psychologist as a springboard for their own thinking. Unfortunately they do not always indicate what or how much they have drawn from these sources.

But it is important that we explore this secular fountainhead. It helps to explain the origin of the teaching in the absence of its explicit biblical support. We can also begin to understand why evangelicals accepted the idea so readily. Finally, such a study is beneficial because, if we can see how those concepts have been developed in the secular world, it will be easier to understand why evangelicals have adopted and stressed certain of the principles.

6

The Self-Theory of Erich Fromm

If secular psychology and not the Bible is the fountainhead of the basic concepts involved in self-love theory, how did this idea develop in the secular world, and how did it pass into evangelicalism? So far we have used terms such as "secular self-theory" to describe the theoretical structure we discussed in the previous chapter. Admittedly, this is an oversimplification. Although the principles of chapter 5 do express the predominant trend in secular self-theory and the almost universal view among evangelicals, there are some who would depart from that formula at various points.

HORNEY'S THEORY

For example, we find that some self-theorists do not hold to the teaching of unconditional lovability. Karen Horney, an earlier self-theorist, concluded that the self-image of a normal person is based on a realistic appraisal of his capacities, including weaknesses and strengths. Horney believed that a self-image not based on realism is characteristic of a neurotic person. She emphasized that the full development of personality is dependent on a self-image that reflects our real self.[1] Therefore, her personality theory involves some sort of a performance basis.

1. Duane Schultz, *Theories of Personality* (Monterey, Calif.: Brooks/ Cole, 1976), p. 79.

71

MASLOW'S CONCEPT

Of a more contemporary vintage is Abraham Maslow, whose background is in behavioral psychology. No doubt this has been at least partially responsible for his tendency to work from a carefully developed data base. Maslow is well-known for his hierarchy of needs, a theory for understanding the various factors that motivate people. One of the motivations that Maslow postulated is the need for esteem. However, he says, "The most stable and therefore most healthy self-esteem is based on deserved respect from others rather than on external fame or celebrity and unwarranted adulation."[2] Here again we see an emphasis on reality as a proper basis for one's self-esteem or self-image. So we find that secular writers are not unanimous in their endorsement of the idea of unconditional lovability and its corollaries. The lack of agreement is especially evident among earlier writers.

FROMM'S INFLUENCE

The concept of unconditional love seemed to come into its own in the work of psychologist Erich Fromm. The impetus he gave to that teaching was phenomenal, though it has not always been fully recognized. In our overview of Fromm's thinking we will discover all of the principles noted in chapter 5. Fromm was a powerful popularizer of these ideas, and part of his success no doubt should be attributed to the fact that he was slightly ahead of the philosophical tide of his day. When existentialism appeared his views were so compatible with it they were latched onto and used.

One of those who drank deeply from the theoretical base provided by Fromm was Carl Rogers. Whether Rogers borrowed directly from Fromm or absorbed his ideas from

2. A. H. Maslow, *Motivation and Personality* (New York: Harper & Row, 1954), p. 91.

the larger environment, they served as a foundation for his client-centered approach to therapy. Rogers took the theorizing of Fromm and put those ideas to practical use. It has been that practical application that has been picked up by evangelicals and squeezed into a more or less biblical mold.

A significant influence in Fromm's thinking is the man-centered foundation from which he builds. That is quite clearly at the heart of his position: "Man is indeed the 'measure of all things.' The humanistic position is that there is nothing higher and nothing more dignified than human existence."[3]

Fromm not only sees man as the highest and most dignified entity in the universe, but also as inherently good and loving. He takes exception to the traditional view that man essentially is egotistical apart from God. Fromm insists that love for one's neighbors is "not a phenomenon transcending man; it is something inherent in and radiating from him."[4] Evidently God is not the source of love, but man is an independent producer of that commodity.

At the heart of Fromm's world view is the concept of love. He sees it as made up of four components: care, responsibility, respect, and knowledge. He defines care as "the active concern for the life and growth of that which we love." He understands responsibility to involve "my response to the needs, expressed or unexpressed, of another human being."[5] Those two terms are quite similar. They seem to focus on will and action and reflect the idea of love we saw in the self-love of William James and in our study of *agapē*.

Respect and knowledge, the second pair in Fromm's

3. Erich Fromm, *Man For Himself* (New York: Holt, Rinehart, and Winston, 1947), p. 13.
4. Ibid., p. 14.
5. Erich Fromm, *The Art of Loving* (New York: Perennial Library, 1956), pp. 22-23.

definition of love, move in a different direction. Respect refers to "the ability to see a person as he is, to be aware of his unique individuality. Respect means the concern that the other person should grow and unfold as he is. . . . If I love the other person, I feel one with him or her but with him *as he is*, not as I need him to be as an object of my use."[6] The critical term in this definition is "as he is." We respect the other person just as we find him, not requiring or even wanting changes. We are to let him be himself and respect him as such. We find the same emphasis in Fromm's definition of knowledge. He believes that knowledge "is only possible when I can transcend the concern for myself and see the other person in his own terms."[7]

In that final definition the phrase "in his own terms" reflects the same basic idea as the earlier phrase "as he is" in Fromm's definition of respect. The implications of those seemingly innocent words are staggering. Fromm is suggesting, or rather requiring, that true love accept the other person "as he is," the principle of unconditional lovability that was seen to be the foundation stone of self-theory. But that is what we might expect to result from Fromm's humanistic presupposition, "Man is the measure of all things." Once man becomes that measure there can be no standard because no one can claim final truth on that basis. Each man becomes his *own* standard and we are caught in the existential dilemma—total relativism.

But does the other person have the right to be loved unconditionally? Fromm responds to this query with an interesting theory: "Love for mankind is looked upon as an achievement which, at best, follows love for an individual or as an abstract concept to be realized only in the future. But love for man cannot be separated from the love for one individual. To love one person productively means to

6. Ibid., pp. 23-24.
7. Ibid., p. 24.

be related to his human core, to him as representing mankind."[8]

Fromm is saying that true love is not superficial in the sense that it does not love only some general unspecified mass known as "mankind." Rather, if love is to be genuine, it must love the individual person in his humanness, at his human core. He believes that all of humanity shares this common core, and therefore if we love one person in this genuine way we will love all people. Conversely, if we exclude one person, if we fail to love him, we do not genuinely love anyone. So here is the second principle of self-theory established clearly; the basis of unconditional love is our humanness. For Fromm, to be human is to be lovable. If I possess a human core I have a right to be loved.

Here too we find support for the third principle, that acceptance is not based on performance. Fromm's theory powerfully defends this idea. He implies that to recognize any basis for love other than the human core is unnecessary. When it comes to genuine love, a person's humanness is all that I am to see. It is to be my total concern.

Of course, Fromm's views make self-love a necessity. If we all partake of that core of humanness, then genuine love must involve *self*-love. Because true love cannot exclude anyone, so it cannot exclude oneself. That also lends support to the idea that self-love does not imply selfishness or pride, since a lack of self-love is really a lack of love for all humanity. Therefore, the *lack* of self-love is selfishness. In addition, because self-love is inseparably bound up with love for all humanity, to love oneself is to love others. So Fromm also substantiates the last two principles of self-theory outlined in chapter 5; namely, that our lovability necessarily calls for self-love, and that such self-love is not selfishness or pride.

Fromm certainly is aware that self-love traditionally has

8. Fromm, *Man*, p. 101.

been viewed as selfishness. He states, "It is assumed that to the degree to which I love myself I do not love others, that self-love is the same as selfishness. This view goes far back in Western thought. Calvin speaks of self-love as 'a pest.' " Not only does he find this inclination in Christianity but also in Freudian psychology. Fromm argues in response, "If it is a virtue to love my neighbor as a human being, it must be a virtue—and not a vice—to love myself, since I am a human being too."[9]

In his development of self-love Fromm made a very significant shift in his definition of love that had vast implications for the future of self-theory. We recall that in his definition of love he defined the terms "care" and "responsibility" in such a way that their essence was will and action. However, when he turned to self-love, he began using terms as "fondness" for oneself.[10] Self-love, then, took on an emotional connotation, so that Fromm was not talking about caring for and being responsible for oneself; it was not *agapē* love or the self-love described by William James. Rather, it was *philia* love and James's "self-feelings" that were in view. The departure by Fromm from his own definition of love shows the looseness of his system.

That is the philosophy of self-love that was seized upon by Carl Rogers, whose influence we will consider next. Fromm gave credence to all the basic presuppositions of self-theory, and thus became a major defender of its foundational expression, "I am lovable, therefore I should love myself."

Because of the foundation of pure humanism that Fromm lays, his views stand on shaky ground. The errors of his starting-point are carried over into his specific teachings. And that is not the only problem with his formulations. Fromm apparently was quite arbitrary in his approach to his theories. Duane Schultz states the case

9. Fromm, *Art*, pp. 48-49.
10. Ibid., p. 51.

concisely: "One cannot find in his (Fromm's) writings any data on which he based his theories."[11] From a platform of humanistic presupposition he made grand pronouncements about man without the data needed to justify his statements. We may ask, "Why did people listen?" Perhaps because he was a man in tune with his times. He said what people wanted to hear, what they wanted to believe.

11. Schultz, p. 100.

7

The Self-Theory of Carl Rogers

Hall and Lindzey in their *Theories of Personality* note
that the most fully-developed formulation of self-theory is
that of Carl Rogers.[1] In our last chapter we saw that
Erich Fromm has been a source of many basic principles
of self-theory. Now we will see those underlying principles
being put to use. Fromm was a formulator, a speculator, a
theorizer; Rogers is a practitioner. He has taken the raw
materials provided by Fromm and molded them into a tool
that can be applied to people. However, Carl Rogers has
achieved something even more revolutionary than that.
He has developed a tool that people can use on *themselves*.

THE SELF-HELP MOVEMENT

In recent years we have seen the advent of a new aspect
of psychology—the self-help movement. In the earlier
years of psychology its application was administered
largely by the professional. The layman stood in awe as
the psychologist or psychiatrist performed his wonders.

But no longer is that true. Today everyone is in on the
act; the self-help movement has swept the country. In almost every bookstore a large section is devoted to its literature. Carl Rogers's approach to therapy lends itself

1. Calvin S. Hall and Gardner Lindzey, *Theories of Personality* (New
York: John Wiley & Sons, 1970), p. 517.

well to this do-it-yourself brand of psychology. As we shall see, it is his formulation primarily that has been adopted by evangelicals. Rogers has molded self-theory into a usable tool. What does that tool look like? The best approach to discussing Rogers will be to take an overview of his basic system and then observe his principles at work in that system.

THE CONTRIBUTION OF ROGERS

Rogers believes that the individual possesses a "self-actualizing" tendency, something like an innate homing device that directs us so that intuitively we know the path that will lead us to self-actualization or fulfillment. Therefore, each person becomes his own best guide. I know what is best for me; the ultimate guide is my self-actualizing tendency, and though you may have the wisdom of the ages at your disposal you cannot improve on that guidance system. That is the reason for Rogers's nondirective approach to counseling. By nondirective we mean that the counselor does not say to the client, "You should do this or you should not do that." Rather, he merely gives the client support through their interpersonal relationship.

The key to fulfillment for the individual is to let himself be guided by his self-actualizing tendency. Here is where the problem comes in. That guidance system can be disrupted. The disruption may begin with the need for acceptance that we all have from significant others. (*Significant* others include parents especially, but also may include teachers, friends, or others with whom the person has a close relationship.) The crucial issue is how the significant other person gives that acceptance. He may do so either conditionally or unconditionally. He may say, "I will accept you if you will behave this way or that way." That is conditional acceptance. Unconditional acceptance, as we have seen, is accepting the person *as he is*, not necessarily requiring change. It requires that the significant other have positive regard for the individual. "In general," Rogers notes, "positive regard is defined as including such attitudes as warmth, liking, respect, sympathy, acceptance."[2]

Rogers sees the individual as a missile that has an internal guidance system taking it to its destination. The system is perfectly designed to do its job, but for some unknown reason it has also been equipped with an override capability that can be controlled by someone on the ground. Now the person on the ground really does not have the capability of hitting the target that the internal guidance system does. Nonetheless, as the ground controller watches the missile, if it appears to him that it is not going quite right he will begin to override the internal system and give the missile directions. The result of all of this is disastrous. The missile is now way off course, and headed in the wrong direction. Here is where the therapist steps in.

As with the missile, the problem for the person begins when acceptance is given on a conditional basis by significant others. The person then can accept himself only if he meets those conditions. So he stops taking his direction from his self-actualizing tendency (his internal guidance system) and begins following the conditions established by others. How is the therapist going to remedy this situation?

Rogers's answer is that the therapist establishes a close relationship with the client, thus becoming a significant other to him. He then communicates to the client that he accepts him unconditionally. Because the client is receiving unconditional acceptance from a significant other, he

2. C. R. Rogers, "A Theory of Therapy, Personality, and Interpersonal Relationship as Developed in the Client-Centered Framework," in *Psychology: A Study of a Science*, ed. S. Koch (New York: McGraw-Hill, 1959), vol. 3, *Formulations of the Person and the Social Context*, p. 208.

now can accept *himself* unconditionally. As a result the client is free from the influence of any conditions of acceptance and can once again be guided by his perfect internal guidance system, his self-actualizing tendency.

Notice that in Rogers's approach he does not develop the principles of self-theory so much as he accepts them as truth and puts them to work.

Beginning with the self-actualizing tendency he displays the same humanism, relativism, and existential tendencies that we found in Fromm, only developed more fully. The heart of his theory is that I know what is best for *me*. No one else does, and no one should try to tell me or to influence me. He should only show me respect and support. Here is a purely individual-centered ethic, and a strong emphasis on unconditional lovability, the first principle of self-theory (see chapter 3).

With Rogers lovability based on humanness also is assumed, and with it the corollary that any performance standard is excluded. In secular thinking those had become "givens." No proof was necessary, so we find the second and third principles of self-theory included as part of the package.

But Rogers not only assumed man's unconditional lovability. His theory asserted that it must be communicated on a continuous basis. To fail to communicate to the other person that he is worthy of love as he is, regardless of performance, is to warp his life-style, stunt his personal growth, and keep him from realizing self-actualization. Conversely, to demonstrate unconditional lovability is to provide the atmosphere in which all of those good things can take root and grow.

Rogers also assumes and strongly supports the fourth and fifth principles of self-theory. In his view unconditional self-love or unconditional self-acceptance is the ultimate trigger that releases the self-actualizing tendency. Therefore, not only may I love myself, but it is a must, a necessity for fulfillment. It also goes without saying that loving myself is not selfishness, but the path both to personal fulfillment and to contributing to society—to others. As I become the self-actualized, well-adjusted, fulfilled person I was intended to be, I can be the neighbor, the friend, the husband, the productive person I was designed to be.

A third concern is Rogers's assumption that unconditional acceptance leads to fulfillment. That is a widely accepted theory today, but many such theories have proven to be false. We have seen that self-love theory is built on a speculative foundation. Furthermore, support for the concept mentioned above is far from evident. That assumption certainly cannot be accepted at face value.

Admittedly, the above analysis has not been exhaustive, nor are we. We are not implying that ideas have flowed directly from Fromm to Rogers to the evangelical world. That would be an oversimplification. Fromm popularized certain ideas that were picked up by others and further developed and dispersed. Carl Rogers is only one of many spokesmen. He seems to have been at the forefront, and as noted at the beginning of the chapter, his formulation of self-theory is quite extensive. Yet there are a hundred other voices echoing the same sentiments, sharing the same principles. That process has continued until it seems those ideas have molded the environment in their own image. What began as speculation three decades ago became theory as it grew and developed. But now, after having heard it so often and from such capable spokesmen, many people have accepted those speculations as truth. And it is that "truth" that evangelicals largely have adopted and absorbed into their own thinking.

8

Self-Love in Evangelical Writings

Some time ago I spoke at a conference whose audience included some pastors. One of the people attending was a woman in her late 20s. She apparently was troubled about something and sought out one of the pastors for counsel. The pastor later discussed the situation with me and concluded by saying, "Her real problem is that she hasn't learned to love herself."

My first reaction was the same as it always is when I hear a pastor or other Christian worker draw that kind of conclusion. On what basis did he make that diagnosis? As a pastor, where did he find that in the Bible? Why didn't he deal with her biblically by speaking about sin, God's forgiveness, and the power of the Holy Spirit to give victory? Later the woman came to see me and it soon became apparent that she had an overt sin problem. Why did the pastor not deal with that?

As I analyzed that pastor's conclusion it was obvious that he was following the secular principle of unconditional lovability. She needed to learn to love herself as she was, and then having learned to love herself she would be able to handle her problems. Here was a pretty clear example of the teaching of Carl Rogers being displayed. However, my pastor friend probably was not borrowing directly from Rogers. There is a good possibility that he has never heard of him, or if he has, that he does not have a working knowledge of Rogers's theories. My friend in all likelihood was reflecting what he had heard and read in evangelical sources. In this chapter we will see how evangelicals have adopted the ideas of self-theory as developed in secular psychology.

A Basic Assumption

We have seen that unconditional love, love based only on *being*, on humanness, was the cornerstone of Fromm's thinking. We noted that Rogers adopted this principle and used it as a basis for his ideas. Likewise we find the same idea as the cornerstone of evangelical self-theory. One writer sums up his book by stating the principle of unconditional love as the basic theme of all that has gone before:

> Now we can see that there are two possible directions for us as we attempt to establish self-esteem. The first direction says: "I can like myself *if* others like me." "I can like myself *if* I live up to my goals and expectations." "I can like myself *if* I succeed in avoiding feelings of guilt and condemnation." In other words, we can choose to build our self-love and self-acceptance on our performance and others' evaluations of us. *We can decide to operate on the basis of a conditional or relative self-concept.*
>
> If we judge ourself on the basis of performance, one half of the people are destined to be losers. They can never measure up. But God didn't assign this type of system. In God's system every one is entitled to dignity and worth. We are entitled to confidence and strength. We are all entitled to a feeling of security and lasting love.[1]

It probably is fair to say that the statement above represents the norm in today's evangelical thinking on unconditional acceptance and the self-love that should result. It is clear that the writer is saying that dignity and worth,

1. Bruce Narramore, *You're Someone Special* (Grand Rapids: Zondervan, 1978), pp. 133-34.

confidence and strength, and a feeling of security and lasting love are the right of all people, or at least of all believers, as they are. That unconditional aspect is even more obvious as one studies the flow of the writer's argument.

THE IMAGE OF GOD

In secular self-theory we found that two bulwarks were used to support the teaching of unconditional lovability. One was the inherent value of humanness, the human core. The other was the negation of performance. In general, evangelical writers follow the same pattern. In fact, almost the full weight of their theory rests on these two principles. They seek to give credence to the first of these two supports, the worth of humanness, by appealing to the theological truth that man was created in the image of God. Narramore concludes:

> When God said, "Let us make man in Our image," (Genesis 1:26), He once and for all provided a basis for human dignity, worth, and value. He sealed forever the fact that every person who walked on earth would have the right to see himself as a creature of worth, value, and importance. . . . No matter how deeply sin mars our image, one fact remains: we are in His image.[2]

Being made in the image of God gives grounds for dignity and worth apart from performance—it provides an unconditional base. Neither the Fall of man nor sin after the Fall has altered that fact. As people created in God's image, our humanness gives us dignity and worth and provides a basis for self-love. Anthony Hoekema concurs with Narramore on that point. Regarding the effects of the Fall he asks:

> Does this mean that man now became of no worth? Nothing could be further from the truth. Even after the fall

2. Ibid., p. 38.

man was still considered to be a creature of infinite worth. Jesus said that one human life is worth more than the whole world (Matt. 16:26). The Scriptures also affirm that even fallen man still bears the image of God (Gen. 9:6; James 3:9).[3]

Many evangelical writers also emphasize that our talents, gifts, and capacities are part of the basis for unconditional self-love. As we look inward we can see those laudable possessions and feel good about ourselves. We can be confident in those gifts and the ability to perform that they give us. In a sense this is a corollary to the idea of worth based on our creation in God's image. One aspect of that creation is the human capacities that are part of our being. Those enablements add to our self-esteem since those qualities are part of what we are.

But what about performance? If sin does not alter the fact that we are in God's image, does performance play a role at all in our lovability? One of the most prominent arguments of evangelical self-love literature is that we must be unconditionally lovable because God's love for us is unconditional. Since our performance does not affect God's love for us, it should not alter our love for ourselves, either. This theme is strongly advocated in the writings of Maurice Wagner. He writes, "True love is voluntary on the part of the lover and unconditional. . . . At the heart of personality is the need to feel a sense of being lovable without having to qualify for acceptance."[4] Wagner's understanding of personality clearly reflects Rogers's theory.

We also see Rogers's influence in Wagner's understanding of the child/parent relationship: "Unconditional love is apparently the only parental attitude that can con-

3. Anthony A. Hoekema, *The Christian Looks at Himself* (Grand Rapids: Eerdmans, 1975), pp. 21-22.
4. Maurice E. Wagner, *The Sensation of Being Somebody* (Grand Rapids: Zondervan, 1975), p. 67.

dition a child to develop an adequate self-concept, for true love is not conditional and it does not change." Wagner sees God as meeting the need for unconditional love that parents can only meet in an imperfect way. He assures us, "God loves us unconditionally, for He is love."[5] This unconditional love of God is at the heart of Wagner's concept of self-love. Neither is he expressing an isolated opinion; rather he is quite representative of evangelical self-love proponents at this point.

Let us recall again the overriding implication of an unconditional, non-performance approach to love and acceptance. It means that nothing we do in any way affects our relationship to God, including either His attitudes or actions toward us. As we shall attempt to demonstrate, that concept is fraught with other implications that are at best difficult to deal with from a biblical perspective.

Perhaps the most concerted effort to tackle that task is made by Bruce Narramore and Bill Counts in their book, *Freedom from Guilt.* Its basic theme is that we as Christians can be totally free from guilt because God does not deal with us on a performance basis. One of their foundational premises is that God *could not* be dealing with us on a performance basis, because if He were, none of us would ever make it and we would all end up feeling guilty all the time: "No matter how noble an act we perform, it is tainted with some degree of selfishness or induced by a wrong motive, or it is never as complete as it should be. Our constant tendency to assert our own will over God's distorts to some degree every aspect of our life."[6]

What, then, is the solution? Since we all live in some degree of sin all of the time, how do we live in freedom from guilt? The answer, as seen by Narramore and Counts, is grace. Narramore makes a concise statement of the case in *You're Someone Special:*

5. Ibid., p. 134.
6. Bruce Narramore and Bill Counts, *Freedom from Guilt* (Irvine, Calif.: Harvest House, 1974), p. 48.

Many of us Christians continue to feel guilty, in spite of the fact that when Christ died on the cross two thousand years ago, He paid the full penalty for all our sins. . . . At the moment Jesus died on the cross, He paid the penalty for our sins once for all. Although we may still *feel* like we deserve punishment for our misdeeds, we don't. He has fully paid for our past sins, our present sins, and even the ones that we haven't thought up yet![7]

As a result, Narramore and Counts observe, "When God looks on us, He sees us 'in Christ.' He doesn't see our dirt. He sees us just as clean and pure as Jesus Christ Himself."[8]

SOME UNANSWERED QUESTIONS

This conclusion generates several questions. The first is whether I should confess my sins since they are already forgiven. Narramore and Counts answer that there is no need of confession as far as our relationship to God is concerned, but we should do so because it is beneficial to our own psychological well-being, that is, it is good catharsis, it helps us to feel cleansed.[9] That approach to confession is one example of the ambivalence we mentioned earlier. Apparently the authors feel the need to hold on to the act of confession, but they also seem to recognize that the idea of confession as normally understood would undermine the principle of unconditional acceptance. So by adjusting our understanding of confession (it is for our psychological benefit), they manage to salvage both confession and unconditional acceptance.

But what about blessings? Won't our sin cause God to withhold His blessing? Narramore and Counts answer, "Under grace, God blesses us unconditionally, then we are encouraged to obey him." Does that mean that regardless

7. Narramore, *Special*, pp. 149-50.
8. Narramore and Counts, p. 81.
9. Ibid., pp. 131-32.

of how sinful we are, God blesses us just the same? What about chastening for sin? Though Narramore and Counts recognize that God does chastise His children, they assert that it is only for our growth and that it is done in love. Therefore, even though we may be living in sin they would advise, "We should never be afraid of God." But if we can sin without loss of blessing and if we need not fear chastening, what is to stop us from sinning? The authors reply, "Under grace, we are accepted first because Christ died for us, then we naturally tend to perform as God wants."[10] Here we see clearly the face of Carl Rogers in evangelical thought. The idea that as we receive unconditional acceptance we automatically will live right is a clear reflection of Rogers's self-actualizing tendency.

Finally, what about my reward? Will I not lose heavenly rewards if I live a life that is weighted down with sin and failure? Here the idea of unconditional acceptance seems to meet theology head-on. Since they cannot deny that a life of disobedience will affect rewards, Narramore and Counts salvage what they can from the situation by reminding us that that loss of rewards should not be looked on as punishment.[11]

It should be noted that the authors do make a strong effort to demonstrate biblically their teaching that the believer's relationship with God is on an unconditional basis. However, we need to recognize that the first three principles of secular self-theory: unconditional lovability, lovability based on humanness, and lovability apart from performance, are also seen to be an integral part of the evangelical formulation.

That brings us to the final pair of principles, the idea that since I am lovable I should love myself, and that such self-love is not selfishness. The first of those is usually assumed by evangelical self-theorists. Little if any attempt

10. Ibid., pp. 96, 72, 95.
11. Ibid., p. 74.

is made to substantiate the principle that lovability should lead necessarily to loving oneself. However, love of self does *not* have to follow lovability. It is one thing to say that we are created in God's image and therefore have worth, or that God loves us on an unconditional basis. It is quite another to assert that I should or must love myself in response. Many evangelicals speak of the psychological need for self-love, but few develop the theological justification for going from "I am lovable" to "I should love myself." The absence of Scriptural teaching at this point is a deterrent to efforts to support this assumption.

The last principle often is stated and dealt with by evangelical writers. Much of what is offered is merely assertion of the fact without an attempt to prove the case exegetically. Another approach is to rehash the arguments of secular psychology. For example, Trobisch reasons, "We cannot give what we do not possess. Only when we have accepted ourselves can we become truly self-less and free from ourselves."[12]

As we consider evangelical teaching it is instructive to note how Carl Rogers's approach has been fitted into a theological framework. He says that we are designed in such a way that we are not fully functioning as long as we receive only conditional acceptance from "significant others." That conditional acceptance causes us to love ourselves on a conditional basis, and we are always striving to meet the conditions rather than be ourselves. Rogers's solution is the therapist, who becomes a significant other and shows us unconditional love. By so doing he helps us love ourselves unconditionally, and then we are free to be ourselves, free to grow and develop, to be productive.

It seems that many evangelical psychologists, perhaps being unaware of Rogers's system, either knowingly or unknowingly have concluded that that is what the Bible

12. Walter Trobisch, *Love Yourself* (Downers Grove: Inter-Varsity, 1976), p. 15.

teaches. In the earthly realm we receive only conditional love. That is why we are unable to function at our best. But God is the perfect therapist; when we are saved He becomes a significant other and provides us with unconditional acceptance, as does the therapist. Then as we recognize our unconditional acceptance we can love ourselves unconditionally. Thus we become free from the conditions that have enslaved us, and are free to be all that God intended us to be. Now I have never read of any evangelical stating the case in quite that way, but an analysis of their approach shows that for many the idea is basic to their system and that for most there is a strong flow in this direction.

There is no doubt that the process of bringing the two worlds together has been exciting for those involved. If the theories of Rogers and others are assumed to be valid, it would seem that God's unconditional love is the answer to man's psychological problems. The implications suggested by that fact are tremendous. It gives evangelicals an approach to personality and therapy that is compatible with a major, widely accepted theory. Secular psychology and evangelical theology have been reconciled. Those truths have been juxtaposed to one another and we have discovered that they are a perfect fit.

But then reality sets in. We must ask ourselves, "Can we take Carl Rogers at face value? Do his teachings really represent a great truth of general revelation, or are they just a passing theory?" Regarding Rogers we have seen already that there is a good reason for concern, reservation, and doubt. However, the union of the Rogerian system with evangelical theology is still in the glow of the honeymoon stage. But as the compatibility of his principles with evangelical theology is analyzed with greater care after the romance of discovery dies down, we feel certain that what appears on the macroscopic level to be a perfect fit will be found on the microscopic level to be quite the opposite.

9

Examining Two Crucial Issues

The Continental Divide is a geological phenomenon that does not readily capture the eye. Most people cross it without even realizing that they have done so. That ridge along the Rocky Mountains marks the dividing line between the water that flows toward the Atlantic Ocean and that which flows toward the Pacific. Though there is not much about the Continental Divide that commends it to us visually, it holds a real fascination for our imaginations. To think (theoretically at least) that a drop of rain landing one inch to the east of that line will begin to wind its course toward the Atlantic, whereas if the wind had blown it a little over an inch to the west it would have headed for the Pacific, is amazing. A small difference in the location of raindrops when they hit the earth will mean all the difference in the world in the direction of their flow and their ultimate destination.

In the same way, when we speak of making fine distinctions in our thinking we are not talking about trivial differences.

Evangelical theology is theocentric (God-centered) at its heart. That fact touches and influences every area of doctrine. However, Rogerian psychology is anthropocentric (man-centered) at its root. The authors of a study entitled *Integration of Psychology and Theology* speak of "Carl Rogers and similar humanistic theoreticians," indicating their recognition that his system is man-centered. They also note that "His writings reflect a strong rejection of the idea that humanity is basically sinful. Instead he focuses on the innate tendency ·toward growth and actualization."[1]

In those two systems (God-centered theology and humanistic psychology) we find something of a Continental Divide. If an idea begins with a humanistic slant, it will flow in that direction until it arrives in the ocean of humanism. Conversely, if we begin with a God-centered concept, as it is developed and expanded it will finally come to rest in that ocean. The question of course is on which side of this divide does the approach of evangelical self-theorists fall? Because small distinctions ultimately will have such major consequences, broad pronouncements made by evangelical writers need to be examined with care. We will consider three such issues here and in chapters 10 and 11.

THE IMAGE OF GOD

Let us begin with a proposition we looked at briefly in chapter 8: man's worth based on his creation in the image of God. That argument involves two major premises. Man has unconditional worth because he is in the image of God, and because he has worth he should love himself. In supporting that concept practically all evangelical writers have dealt with the first premise, but the second aspect of the argument has been too often ignored or assumed. That, however, is to take far too much for granted. Even if we agree that man has worth because he is in God's image, the question remains, does that give him the right to feel *good* about himself? Is that really a legitimate basis for self-esteem?

The Scriptural response to that assumption seems to be clear. Jeremiah states it emphatically: "Thus says the LORD, 'Let not a wise man boast of his wisdom, and let not the mighty man boast of his might, let not a rich man boast of his

1. John D. Carter and Bruce Narramore, *The Integration of Psychology and Theology* (Grand Rapids: Zondervan, 1979), pp. 37, 35.

riches; but let him who boasts boast of this, that he understands and knows Me, that I am the LORD who exercises lovingkindness, justice, and righteousness on earth; for I delight in these things,' declares the LORD" (Jeremiah 9:23-24).

Notice that the Lord is not contesting the claim of the man in question. He is not saying, "Why are you making an empty boast? You are not rich or wise or mighty." The Lord is saying, even if you possess those attributes do not let them be your source of glorying. He also does not say "stop glorying." The problem is that the man has chosen the wrong object for his boasting. Further, the passage does not tell us to glory in ourselves *first*, and then as we develop an adequate self-image we will be able to glory in the Lord. Finally, the Lord does not say, "Give credit where credit is due. You take the share of glory that is due to you, and then give Me what is Mine." Rather He is saying even if you have worth, a basis for a good self-esteem, your boast should not be in yourself but in Him.

Jeremiah is not just speaking here of outward expression. He does not condone the attitude of self-esteem as long as it is not talked about. Rather he is dealing with a heart attitude of humility. We should not have a heart filled with self-glory, but with praise for the Lord. And this passage is not an isolated theme in Scripture. It represents the mainstream of biblical thought. Not only is the Bible silent when it comes to any encouragement to "feel good" about ourselves, but one of its major themes is that we should not boast in self but in the Lord. Paul echoes Jeremiah in 1 Corinthians 1:31 when he writes, "Let him who boasts, boast in the LORD."

But why must this be so? If I am wise or mighty or whatever, why should I not take pride in it? Why should I not feel good about myself and esteem myself for it? Paul answers that question in 1 Corinthians 4:7: "For who regards you as superior? And what do you have that you did not receive? But if you did receive it, why do you boast as if you had not received it?" His principle reminds us that we are not responsible for our talents and gifts; everything we have has been bestowed on us—and the giver obviously is God. We did nothing to bring ourselves into existence. Paul's pronouncement recalls the teaching of Psalm 100:3: "Know that the LORD Himself is God; It is He who has made us, and not we ourselves." Therefore, whatever worth we have is not of our own doing, but is from God, and so our boast should be directed toward Him.

One of the major arguments used by evangelical writers to demonstrate that we should feel good about ourselves is the Scripture that tell us we are "fearfully and wonderfully made" (Psalm 139:14). But the real point of the verse, expressed in the first phrase, is often overlooked by these enthusiasts. The full verse says, "I will give thanks to *Thee*, for I am fearfully and wonderfully made; wonderful are *Thy* works, and my soul knows it very well" (italics added). The psalmist seeks to give glory to *God* for His magnificence displayed in creation. Yet the evangelical theorist seems to alter the verse so that it says, "I will praise *me*, for I am fearfully and wonderfully made." Although both views start at the same point, that of human worth and capacity, that which is a great theocentric truth in Scripture has become a man-centered teaching at the hands of both secular and evangelical self-theorists. What God intended to be a source of praise to Himself has become malformed so as to become a human basis for self-adoration.

What is at the heart of these diametrically opposed responses? The answer lies in the issue of *dependence* versus *autonomy*. The theocentric view recognizes the truth of 1 Corinthians 4:7, that I owe my "being" to the Lord. That not only involves the fact that He created me at some point in the past, but also the recognition that He sustains my life on a moment-by-moment basis. Likewise my talents and abilities are not self-made but God-given. But what is more, their use is dependent on the Lord both in the physical sense of having life, breath, and energy to exercise them, and in the spiritual sense of needing the inflow of God's Spirit for their effective use. Thus "being" in the image of God is not something that I possess independently, and the worth that springs from that being should not be ascribed to the image, but to the Source that gave and sustains it.

The existential view of man, however, sees him as independent and autonomous. In its rejection of systems existentialism is unconcerned either about origins or any theories regarding daily preservation and sustenance. What I know for certain by immediate experience is that I am here and I am me, and if I like what I see there is no one to feel good about but me. If I accomplish anything I have only myself to like for what I have done.

So autonomy, and thus self-love, is a natural for the humanistic psychologist with his existential tendencies, but what about the evangelical psychologist? His attempt to embrace self-love with its implied autonomy and at the same time hold to theocentric theology creates an ambivalence in his thinking.

But to carry the case a step further, let us forget about origins for a moment. Then it might be argued, "Even if I was created by God, that is a thing of the past. Regardless of how all this came into being, I still have gifts and capacities that I can use and feel good about." But that is just a special case for the "image of God" argument. We have worth because of the way we are made. Only now the focus is on man's capacity to do, to perform. It does appear that that argument offers more hope for an autonomous basis for worth, because *we* are the ones who possess, develop, and decide to use our talents on a daily basis.

That search for autonomous worth in our capabilities and gifts is apparent in Narramore's discussion of the person who sang a solo in church. After the service, when someone expressed appreciation for the ministry, the person responded, "It wasn't me. It was the Lord who did it." Narramore takes exception to this reply. He asks: "Now wait a minute. Who did it? You were singing with the voice that God created you with, but it is not like if you'd set a robot up there you would have heard the same message, you see. If that guy's a rank pagan he may be singing in the New York Met because he's got a voice."[2]

The implication here is that the singer's statement is wrong, and that his ministry really was autonomous. But that approach overlooks a great scriptural truth. It misses the point of our need for God's constant support in every aspect of our lives on a moment-by-moment basis. It forgets that as the person was singing the air that he breathed, the platform he stood on, even the heart that kept him alive were all upheld by the "word of His power" (Hebrews 1:3). To give God the glory was the only reasonable response for the soloist.

Narramore reflects some ambivalence on this matter of human abilities, however. Although he wants to establish inherent worth for man, he realizes that God's power and glory must be given place also. So in *You're Someone Special* he concludes the section on humility with the statement, "Although we can accomplish many things, we cannot function at our best without a recognition of our need of Him."[3] He cannot seem to bring himself to say what Christ said in John 15:5: "For apart from Me you can do nothing." In fact, when he quotes John 15:5 in the same volume he includes the rest of the verse but curiously leaves out that last phrase.[4]

Illustrations of this kind of ambivalence can also be found at numerous places in the writings of other

2. Bruce Narramore, "The Christian's Self-Esteem," lecture given at Dallas Theological Seminary, Dallas, Tex., 31 October 1975. Cassette #715, Dallas Seminary Library.
3. Bruce Narramore, *You're Someone Special* (Grand Rapids: Zondervan, 1978), p. 62.
4. Ibid., p. 131.

evangelicals. They reflect the struggle of those writers who are seeking to find autonomous worth for man and yet hold on to the truth that God is the worthy object of our praise. In order for that worth to be inherently his, man's gifts must function autonomously; they must be operative apart from the work of God. But that ignores the fact that not only did God create us, but we are totally dependent on Him for our life, breath, and everything else.

One of the crucial distinctions between being God and being in the image of God is that of autonomy versus dependence. The Creator God is not dependent on His creation. Rather He is totally independent, whereas all else is dependent on Him. That thought is reflected in the primary name of God, Yahweh, that apparently has its root in the Hebrew verb "to be." Thus when Moses asked regarding His name, the Lord responded, "I AM WHO I AM" (Exod. 3:14). One of the major implications of that name is that He is the self-existent God, and as such the cause, the ground of the existence of every other creature. The root error of existentialism is that it gives the individual the autonomy that belongs only to Yahweh.

This independence of God as contrasted with the dependence of man is not restricted to creation, however. The old error of Deism certainly was not derived from Scripture. The Bible gives no indication that the world was designed to get along without God. The fact is that He upholds all things by the Word of His power. Furthermore, it would be a mistake to limit God's activity in the universe today to mere preservation. James 1:17 informs us that "every good thing bestowed and every perfect gift is from above, coming down from the Father of lights, with whom there is no variation, or shifting shadow." Here both the finite verb "is" and the participle "coming down" are present tense, indicating continuing action. God did not stop giving at creation, but everything in the world today that has any merit or value has God as its source.

The Christian, of course, is heir of a special measure of God's grace as one who is His child and the recipient of resurrection life through the new birth. We are totally dependent on Him for the production of anything of worth in this supernatural life to which we are called. Man in the *image* of God is not capable of being the *source* of anything of value. Rather, being in God's image gives him the special capacity to be a *channel* for the life of God and as such, to produce that which has worth. Christ made that clear in His discourse on the vine and the branches: "I am the vine, you are the branches; he who abides in Me, and I in him, he bears much fruit; *for* apart from Me you can do nothing" (John 15:5, italics added).

The view of man as having autonomous worth leads to an error in a very practical area of Christian living. It produces a somewhat misplaced confidence. Narramore says, "Next to the knowledge that God created us stands another pillar of our self-esteem—the awareness of our abilities and a sense of inner strength."[5]

But the thrust of the Bible seems to be in the opposite direction. Time after time we see the Lord bringing people to the end of their own strength, their human capacities, so that He can demonstrate how dependent they are on Him. Abraham made a last-ditch effort through human capacity with Hagar and Ishmael, but to his regret and recognition that this was not God's program. God was waiting to show him that He was *El Shaddai*, the God who works when people come to the end of themselves.

Moses' human efforts were only able to bury one Egyptian in his attempt to bring relief to his people in their bondage. God needed to take him aside and teach him not to trust in human capacity but in Himself, the great "I AM" who begins working when human abilities are exhausted and human hope is gone. God is teaching us the same lesson with David and Goliath. Goliath came out with sword,

5. Ibid., p. 62.

spear, and shield, but David said, "I come to you in the name of the LORD of hosts, the God of the armies of Israel, whom you have taunted" (1 Samuel 17:45). From the standpoint of human capacities, David did not stand a chance.

We are reminded of this truth again in Zechariah 4:6. "Not by might nor by power, but by My Spirit, says the LORD of hosts." Paul likewise spoke of casting away human confidence in exchange for the power of God when he testified, "Most gladly, therefore, I will rather boast about my weaknesses, that the power of Christ may dwell in me" (2 Corinthians 12:9). It is a serious theological error to see confidence in our abilities as a hallmark of mature faith, and then to view that confidence as the basis of self-esteem. What a drastic departure that is from Paul's thinking when he declared: "Not that we are adequate in ourselves to consider anything as coming from ourselves, but our adequacy is from God" (2 Corinthians 3:5).

How good it is to trade self-confidence for God-confidence. The problem with the former is seen in the story of Saul and Goliath. Saul was head and shoulders above everyone in Israel. He had a real basis for human confidence. Then one day he met Goliath. As we read of the account of Goliath's challenges to the armies of Israel, we realize that the most likely Israelite from a human perspective to fight this giant was Saul. But he who had depended on human greatness found himself in a situation with a greater human. How embarrassing those days must have been to Saul as Israel looked to him to act. No wonder he was so eager to meet David and grasp at any relief from his humiliating situation.

Here is the problem with self-confidence. There is always that person who is bigger, more gifted, quicker with the answer, always that situation beyond our abilities. How much better to be a David than a Saul. Rather than basing our confidence on our limited abilities, how much better to draw on the infinite resources of Yahweh. Then we need not worry about meeting a modern-day Goliath because we have a foundation for limitless confidence.

Perhaps one of our greatest needs as evangelicals is to see that self-theory really does not give, it takes. So often people seem to feel that to give up self-love is to come out on the short end. Here we see that nothing could be farther from the truth. How much better to trade in all that we are for all that God is as the source of our confidence. From the scriptural perspective man cannot be viewed as autonomous, either in his existence or his ability to perform.

In Daniel 4 we find that lesson being taught to Nebuchadnezzar. We are reminded of his words: "Is this not Babylon the great, which I myself have built as a royal residence by the might of my power and for the glory of my majesty?" (Daniel 4:30). God's judgment for that evaluation came "While the word was in the king's mouth. . . ." God's judgment evidently was a result of that proclamation of autonomous accomplishment. And what was the result of God's chastening work in the heart of Nebuchadnezzar? His evaluation changed drastically from the previous emphasis on himself to a new emphasis on God. "Now I Nebuchadnezzar praise, exalt, and honor the King of heaven, for all His works are true and His ways just, and He is able to humble those who walk in pride" (Daniel 4:37). Nebuchadnezzar saw that accomplishment should not and must not lead to self-esteem, but to the exaltation of the Lord who is its author. If the Lord was so insistent that a pagan king assign all glory to its rightful recipient, how much more should we, His children, take care to do the same? And since in that case an earthly kingdom was in view, how much more should we, as heirs of a heavenly kingdom, be careful to give God all the glory for those things that He has imparted to us?

Whatever our worth may be, whatever capacities we may have, whatever may be accomplished through them, as we

recognize that everything of worth finds its ultimate source
in God and depends on Him for life and meaning and fruit-
fulness, the appropriate response is not self-esteem but
adoration of the God who is the source of all.

THE ARGUMENT FROM REDEMPTION

But the argument from our creation in God's image is
not the only one by which evangelical proponents of self-
love seek to establish human worth so as to have a basis
for self-esteem. In the writings of a broad representation
of those authors we discover that we can base our worth
and therefore our self-love on the doctrine of redemption.
One spokesman puts it this way: "The continuing worth of
man after the fall is particularly evident in the Bible's
teaching on redemption. . . . Surely God would not give
His Son for creatures He considered to be of little
worth."[6]

Again, however, that argument is questionable at best.
Christ is viewed as dying for man because man has worth;
the atonement is based on and motivated by man's value.
But the problem with that view is that it undermines the
biblical teaching of the grace of God. It weakens God's
grace as the foundation of our redemption.

We may illustrate the fallacy of basing human worth on
redemption in this way. When we go shopping we seek to
get "our money's worth." This we rightly consider our just
due. And we succeed when we conclude that what was
purchased was equal in value to the amount we paid. However, at that exchange there is no grace shown, nor would
we expect it. The merchant got his money, and we got our
merchandise. That is only business as usual, a fair deal.

The idea is simply this: In business the price paid is related to the worth of the merchandise. But with the principle of grace there is *no* relationship between the pur-

6. Anthony A. Hoekema, *The Christian Looks at Himself* (Grand
Rapids: Eerdmans, 1975), p. 22.

chase price and the value of that which is purchased. When Scripture speaks of redemption, it describes the greatest act of grace the world has ever known. By no means does it seek to equate the purchase price—the precious blood of Christ—with that which was purchased—our souls. To attempt to do so is to fail to see the grace of God for what it is. Instead it is to make God merely one of the parties in a business transaction. To virtually assign man a worth equal to the blood of Christ is to go far beyond what the Bible warrants, no matter how understandable the motive.

Of course the question is, Did Christ die for us because we were worthy or despite the fact that we were *un*worthy? The whole concept of biblical love and grace seems to favor the latter. The message of Romans 5:8 and 1 John 4:10 is that God loved the unlovely. The atonement is not a demonstration of the worth of man but of the grace of God. Seeking to focus on our worth as the reason for the atonement distorts the Scriptural account of redemption. In that light the statement of one self-love advocate becomes rather astounding: "There must be something truly wonderful about us if he (God) can love and accept us so readily."[7] One wonders how God's acceptance of us can be viewed as being accomplished "so readily" when it required the greatest sacrifice God could make to bring it about. Did not Jesus agonize in the garden as He faced the awful reality of the cross? That author's view seems to overlook the sufferings of Christ that were necessary to bring man to the place that he could be rightly related to God. We should be painfully aware that God's acceptance of us did not communicate that there is "something truly wonderful about us," but rather that there is everything truly wonderful about *Him*, especially His love and grace.

Scripture underscores the truth that the atonement was

7. Cecil G. Osborne, *The Art of Learning to Love Yourself* (Grand Rapids: Zondervan, 1976), p. 137.

a demonstration of God's grace apart from our worth. That is the apostle Paul's point in 1 Corinthians 1:26-29 where he reminds us, "For consider your calling, brethren, that there were not many wise according to the flesh, not many mighty, not many noble; but God has chosen the foolish things of the world to shame the wise; and God has chosen the weak things of the world to shame the things which are strong, and the base things of the world and the despised, God has chosen, the things that are not, that He might nullify the things that are, *that no man should boast before God*" (italics added). The emphasis is on the unworthiness of the objects of God's gracious calling.

Some seek to contest the conclusions drawn above by arguing that the doctrine of grace pertains to man's sin and not to his worth. Grace is a reflection on our sinfulness, our unworthiness in performance, but not our basic worth as human beings. But to assert that is to say that finite man would be ontologically worthy of the life of the Son of God. That conclusion contradicts John the Baptist's word to the Pharisees and Sadducees: "For I say to you, that God is able from these stones to raise up children to Abraham" (Matthew 3:9). Is this to say then that man has no worth? No, not at all. The issue is the *basis* of that worth.

But what is that basis? The answer probably has been stated most concisely by Martin Luther in his fourth thesis: "God does not love us because we are valuable; we are valuable because God loves us."[8]

For the source of his value, man must not look *inward;* he must look *upward.* The point is not who or what we are, but who God is, that is, He is a loving and gracious God. The constant inward look of evangelical self-theory misses what Martin Luther did not miss. Our claim to worth is not grounded in ourselves but in God.

Our search for worth should cause us to rest in the truth

8. John R. W. Stott, "Must I Really Love Myself?" *Christianity Today,* 5 May 1978, p. 35.

that its source and constant basis is not in the creature but in the Creator. Whether we look at creation or the cross, we are made to realize that our focus should not be on ourselves but on the great God who made and redeemed us.

10

Is Our Acceptance Unconditional?

Having considered the case for self-love from the standpoint of creation and redemption, let us examine more closely the argument that an individual can feel good about himself regardless of performance because God accepts him unconditionally. We saw earlier that, existentially speaking, it is my right to do whatever I please. And whatever that may be, I still deserve to be accepted by others. If they will not accept me on those terms, they are guilty of trying to impose their standards, opinions, and values on me. One evangelical psychologist's approach to child-rearing illustrates well the principle of unconditional acceptance in action. Of course, the parent must do the unconditional accepting, while the child gets to live more "existentially."

Consider by way of illustration the following paragraph:

> Children need to respect their parents. But respect must be earned through respectful living. It cannot be "won" through power! A child may learn that he can't "sass" his parents without getting clobbered. So he stops sassing or retreats a few feet before making his remarks. But what has been accomplished? The child fears his parents' power but inwardly has even less respect. How can he respect an adult who is angered by a childish attack on his self-esteem? He really can't. The way to win respect is to hear your child out. If he is upset, let him tell you. If you allow expression of his

true feelings, you are showing respect. When you respect your child he returns the favor.[1]

As we look at the situation a bit closer, what is the author really saying? Though he begins with the fact that children need to respect their parents, it is obvious that he does not -mean they must be *taught* (with discipline if necessary) to act with respect toward their parents. Rather, as the parent accepts the child unconditionally, apparently no matter what he does, parental respect will somehow grow naturally within the child. That is a pure Rogerian approach to the task of raising children.

On the other side of the ledger, however, parents are seen to have few rights. The parent's attempt to correct the child is caricatured by the term "clobber[ing]." It is intimated that the parent did a foolish thing, since obviously it did no good. In addition, the parent is accused of being motivated in that act not by a desire to train his child but by his wounded self-esteem! The message seems to be that a parent's only right is to show unconditional acceptance. In fact, the author is quite candid at this point: ". . . we can make our child feel his immense worth by showing him our unconditional love. This means we accept our children fully, no matter how they act."[2]

But any arrangement by which one person constantly gives unconditional acceptance to another is unworkable in any absolute sense. The theory can never be fully put into practice; it must give way to the realities of life in its application. The only way any person-to-person relationship can survive is with at least some responsibilities on both sides. There must be some conditions of acceptance.

OUR ACCEPTANCE BEFORE GOD

According to evangelical self-theory, in the believer's re-

1. Bruce Narramore, *Help! I'm a Parent* (Grand Rapids: Zondervan, 1972), p. 42.
2. Ibid., p. 116.

lationship to God we are faced with what seems to be a
striking reversal of roles. Man gets to be the existential
"god" and God is seen as serving in the role of the one who
does the unconditional accepting. The essence of that approach is an adaptation of Rogers's basic structure, with
God in the role of the "significant other" whose unconditional acceptance is the key to our positive self-image or
self-love.

As we saw earlier, some attempt to carry that approach to
its limit. Beginning with the idea that sins past, present, and
future are covered by the atonement, they teach that when
God looks on us He sees only the righteousness of Christ.
Thus, because we are unconditionally accepted, our actions
have no bearing on God's attitudes and actions toward us. So
the confession is not necessary from God's perspective, only
from ours, and only as a means of catharsis—to help us *feel*
cleansed. Though God does chasten at times, He does so
lovingly and for our benefit, so there is never any need to
fear His chastening hand. In addition, apparently sin does
not hinder God's blessing on our lives. His relationship with
us is on a totally unconditional basis.

There is, however, a good deal of scriptural evidence that
calls those conclusions into question. The matter of God's
present blessing may be a good starting point. Compare the
statement "under grace God blesses us unconditionally,
then we are encouraged to obey Him"[3] with 1 Peter 3:10-12:
"For let him who means to love life and see good days refrain
his tongue from evil and his lips from speaking guile. And let
him turn away from evil and do good; let him seek peace and
pursue it. For the eyes of the Lord are upon the righteous,
and His ears attend to their prayer, but the face of the Lord
is against those who do evil." That admonition is by no means
unique in Scripture. In the same book Peter says, "All of
you, clothe yourselves with humility toward one another, for

3. Bruce Narramore and Bill Counts, *Freedom from Guilt* (Irvine,
   Calif.: Harvest House, 1974), p. 96.

God is opposed to the proud, but gives grace to the humble" (1 Peter 5:5).

Other aspects of the teaching of unconditional acceptance are also swimming upstream against a strong tide of biblical teaching. Does the Christian not need to confess his sins except for his own psychological benefit? First John 1:9 seems to point in the opposite direction. There has been an attempt in recent years to interpret that verse in a way that excludes our need of confession. For example, Peter Gillquist notes that the word "confess" in 1 John 1:9 means ". . . to agree with God concerning. . . ." The agreement in question is believed to be, "First, that it is sin; secondly, that it is forgiven already because God says it is!"[4]

This interpretation of the verse is problematic in that it does not agree with the statement of the passage. John does not tell us to recognize that we are already forgiven. The verse would make no sense if it read, "If you agree with God that He has already forgiven your sins, then He will forgive them." That understanding places the forgiveness both before and after our agreement. God is said to forgive that which has already been forgiven by Him. That creates a logical fallacy.

THE NEED FOR CONFESSION

But if Christ has already died for our sins, what is the purpose of confession in 1 John 1:9? We need to recognize that in our relationship with God justification is not the end of the matter. That involves man's relationship with God as our Judge. The person who has been justified no longer needs to stand before God on that basis. He does, however, have a new relationship with God as *Father*. Though God will never sit as Judge in regard to the eternal destiny of His children, that does not mean that He is blind or indifferent to their sins.

4. Peter E. Gillquist, *Love Is Now* (Grand Rapids: Zondervan, 1970), p. 64.

Lewis Sperry Chafer states the case as follows:

> It is evident that the divine forgiveness of the believer is household in its character. It contemplates not the once-for-all forgiveness of the one who already and permanently is a member of the household and family of God. Vital union with God, which is secured by Christ for the believer, has not been and cannot be broken. This renewal is unto fellowship and communion with God.[5]

With reference to 1 John 1:9, Zane C. Hodges explains: "As a Father, God is free to set the terms on which His children shall commune with Him and His refusal to commune with the sinning child until confession has occurred is transparently a divine prerogative. Hence forgiveness, in this context of thought, relates to the restoration of broken fellowship within the household of God."[6]

The view of 1 John 1:9 that appears to have the greatest exegetical support is that which holds that the Christian must confess his sins in order to have forgiveness and fellowship in his family relationship with God. That verse and other passages lead us to conclude that our relationship with God does include a conditional element, not involving our security, but affecting fellowship, blessing, God's use of us in ministry, and eternal reward.

That fact is evident, for example, in the New Testament teaching on the qualifications of elders. In Titus 1:6-10 the list of requisites does not focus on capabilities needed for the job, but on performance, that is, how the person has lived. The Holy Spirit is saying, "If your life does not measure up, you are not qualified to be an elder." That hardly sounds unconditional and non-performance related.

The fact that God's use of the Christian is conditioned on godly living does not apply only to elders, however. Paul

5. Lewis Sperry Chafer, *Systematic Theology*, 8 vols. (Dallas, Tex.: Dallas Seminary, 1948), 2:337-38.
6. Zane C. Hodges, "Fellowship and Confession in I John 1:5-10," *Bibliotheca Sacra* 129, no. 513 (January-March 1972):57.

exhorts Timothy: "Let every one who names the name of the Lord abstain from wickedness. Now in a large house there are not only gold and silver vessels, but also vessels of wood and of earthenware, and some to honor and some to dishonor. Therefore, if a man cleanses himself from these things, he will be a vessel for honor, sanctified, useful to the Master, prepared for every good work" (2 Timothy 2:19b-21).

Another area in which our relationship with God is conditional is that of eternal reward. In several places the apostle Paul speaks of his concern over his reward. It seems that he was intent on making every day count for eternity. So he is fearful about the Galatians "that perhaps I have labored over you in vain" (Galatians 4:11b). But he rejoices to the Thessalonians: "For who is our hope or joy or crown of exultation? Is it not even you, in the presence of our Lord Jesus Christ at His coming?" (1 Thessalonians 2:18). Paul was also concerned about the reward of the Philippians: "Not that I seek the gift itself, but I seek for the profit which increases to your account" (Philippians 4:17).

Apparently it makes a great deal of difference to God and to us how we live. It affects our fellowship with Him, our suitability for service, His blessing on our lives, and much more. Our relationship with God is conditional in many vital respects. We can come to the end and look back on a life of failure and defeat, or we can be like Paul, whose final testimony was, "I have fought the good fight, I have finished the course, I have kept the faith; in the future there is laid up for me the crown of righteousness, which the Lord, the righteous Judge, will award me on that day; and not only to me, but also to all who have loved His appearing" (2 Timothy 4:7-8).

11

The Issue of Performance

Walter Trobisch begins his book *Love Yourself* by relating the story of a counseling session he had while at a university in northern Europe. The counselee was a beautiful Scandinavian girl whose problem was that she came from a "tight-laced religious family" where she had learned that to have any self-appreciation at all was sinful. Trobisch offers the following account of his approach to the problem.

> We asked her to stand up and take a look in the mirror. She turned her head away. With gentle force I held her head so that she had to look into her own eyes. She cringed as if she were experiencing physical pain.
>
> It took a long time before she was able to whisper, though unconvinced, the sentence I asked her to repeat, "I am a beautiful girl."[1]

In considering this dramatic scene I am left with one simple question—what if she were unattractive? When Trobisch brought her to the mirror, what would he have told her to say then?

An obvious response by a self-theorist might be that we do not build our self-esteem on our outward appearance, but on the more profound inner aspects of our personality. But therein lies the very root of our problem. What about those

1. Walter Trobisch, *Love Yourself* (Downers Grove: Inter-Varsity, 1976), pp. 7-8.

inner aspects of our personhood? What if we were to take a different mirror, the Word of God (James 1), and hold it up to our hearts and lives? What would we see? Even the Christian has to admit that the reflection is not always appealing.

Performance Does Matter

We have already discussed the fact that performance *does* matter to God and therefore should be a concern of ours as well. That conclusion then confronts us with the issue of how well we perform. Since what we do on a daily basis is so important, how should this matter of performance relate to our professed need for a healthy self-image?

Anthony Hoekema gives a larger place to performance than do most evangelical self-theorists. He affirms, "Though the Christian self-image is rooted in divine grace, one cannot expect to continue to enjoy a positive self-image if he is living irresponsibly."[2] Though Hoekema recognizes that failure as a possibility, he does not see it as the norm. He seeks to demonstrate that the life of the believer is essentially victory-oriented and that as the Christian looks inside he can feel good about what he sees. As a summary to one chapter he states ". . . we who are in Christ are to view ourselves as new creatures who are now in the strength of His Spirit *living a life of victory*" (italics added).[3]

But could Hoekema have written that to the Corinthians? We realize that the Christian has the *potential* to live in victory, but we cannot fail to observe the difference between potential and reality. Hoekema would like to draw that picture of the (apparently continuous) victorious Christian life as a basis for a positive self-image. But we are confronted with the question, "Is that where we always are? Is that where I lived yesterday, or may be living today?" If the

2. Anthony A. Hoekema, *The Christian Looks at Himself* (Grand Rapids: Eerdmans, 1975), p. 99.
3. Ibid., p. 60.

answer is ever negative, it seems that my self-image would fluctuate dramatically and at times actually work against me.

Hoekema does admit, "In this present life we shall never get beyond the need for daily confession of sin, as Christ Himself taught us in the fifth petition of the Lord's Prayer." He seeks to reconcile the conflict by arguing, "Granted, the believer may lose many a battle, particularly when he relies on his own strength instead of looking to the Lord. But one may lose many battles and still win the war. And when one is in Christ the final outcome is never in question."[4]

But Hoekema's argument is somewhat confusing. What does he mean when he says we may still "win the war"? If he means getting to heaven, that is a settled issue for the believer. But there is more to the Christian life and its outcome than that. If he's referring to the potential every believer has for a life of fruitful maturity and victory, his conclusion is far from certain.

Though the Bible does not give us statistics on the matter, we do find scriptural evidence that many are not enjoying spiritual victory. We already mentioned the church at Corinth. The Galatians had their own set of problems. And even the spiritual Philippians had a little squabble in their midst that assures us that they were not too far removed from our churches in the twentieth century. The seven churches of Revelation 2 and 3 do not help the average either.

We could shift our focus from churches to individuals with the same results. There even appears to be a serious problem with Paul's closest disciple Timothy, that we read about in 2 Timothy. That book was written at the end of Paul's ministry, when we might have expected Timothy to have realized considerable maturity. If Timothy was having problems, after being the prize student in Paul's discipleship program, then what about the "average" Christian?

4. Ibid.

Paul himself fought so as not to be a castaway (1 Corinthians 9:27). He was not referring to his eternal destiny but to victory and usefulness in life for the Lord. To his credit, Hoekema does recognize the reality of spiritual struggle, but it is still questionable whether we are to look inward for a positive self-image. The Bible does not encourage us to do so. Even the most spiritual Christian cannot stand before the mirror of the Word of God with great confidence and say, "I am a beautiful person."

The great theologian, Charles Hodge, reflects:

> . . . the most advanced believer has need, as long as he continues in the flesh, daily to pray for the forgiveness of sins. . . . All feel, and all are bound to acknowledge that they are sinners whenever they present themselves before God; all know that they need constantly the intervention of Christ, and the application of His blood to secure fellowship with the Holy One. As portrayed in Scripture, the inward life of the people of God to the end of their course in this world, is a repetition of conversion. It is a continued turning unto God; a constant renewal of confession, repentance, and faith; a dying unto sin, a living unto righteousness. This is true of all saints, patriarchs, prophets, and apostles of whose inward experience the Bible gives us any account. . . . There are no forms of worship, no formulas for private devotion in any age or part of the Church, which do not contain confession of sin and prayer for forgiveness. The whole Christian Church with all its members prostrates itself before God saying, "Have mercy upon us miserable sinners."[5]

As to the basis of that great need for confession, Hodge affirms:

> We appeal to the conscience of every believer. He knows that he is a sinner. He never is in a state which satisfies his own conviction as to what he ought to be. He may call his deficiencies infirmities, weaknesses, and errors, and may refuse to

5. Charles Hodge, *Systematic Theology*, 3 vols. (Grand Rapids: Eerdmans, 1968), 3:245-47, 250.

call them sins. But this does not alter the case. Whatever
they are called, it is admitted that they need God's pardoning
mercy.[6]

Hodge reminds us of something we are all well aware of,
that even as God's children our battle with sin is a great
struggle. We think of Paul's longing in Romans 8:22-23: "For
we know that the whole creation groans and suffers the
pains of childbirth together until now. And not only this, but
also we ourselves, having the first fruits of the Spirit, even
we ourselves groan within ourselves, waiting eagerly for our
adoption as sons, the redemption of our body." How well we
relate to Isaiah who, when in the presence of God's holiness,
cried, "Woe is me, for I am ruined! Because I am a man of
unclean lips, and I live among a people of unclean lips; for my
eyes have seen the King, the LORD of hosts" (Isaiah 6:5).

We certainly do not mean to overlook the forgiveness of
God, but even though we can rest in the confidence that we
are forgiven we still have to live with the scars that have
been left by our sinfulness. There are broken homes, missed
opportunities, wasted years, ruined health, drug-distorted
minds, lost fortunes, years of grief that can never be re-
tracted, and an array of lesser scars left in the wake of the
sins of daily living. Added to that painful list is the discredit
we have brought on the name of the Lord by un-Christlike
behavior.

Neither are we ignoring our wonderful position in
Christ, and the benefits that are ours because we are in
Him. But that does not negate the reality of our performance and its effect on our relationship with the Lord and
with others, and its impact on our own lives as well.

If we are looking at performance as a good source of
healthy self-love, we must face the disturbing fact that our
performance is marred. The greatest problem I have in
trying to establish a good self-image on the basis of performance is me. As I look inward I see much that I do not like:

6. Ibid., p. 250.

wrong attitudes and motives, weaknesses, and inclinations to sin. Then as I look at the flaws in performance those defects produce I have a difficult time standing before the mirror of God's Word and saying, "I am a beautiful person."

12

The Peril of Self-Love

Have you ever stopped to think what it would sound like if a person verbalized what self-theory taught him to think? Let us take Trobisch's Norwegian girl, for example. Suppose that he was successful in helping her to gain a full appreciation of her attractiveness. That night as she was dining out with her boyfriend she might share with him her discovery. "Nels, today I came to realize that I am a very beautiful girl. Now I see that I have a gorgeous face, lovely eyes, and a vivacious smile."

Or imagine George strolling into the country club after winning the town golf tournament and saying, "It feels so great to know that you are good. Actually, I've always known that I am a rather fine golfer. I certainly do play a superb game. I really feel good about myself."

It might be argued that it is acceptable to esteem yourself, as long as you do not talk about it. But if it is acceptable to think such thoughts, why cannot they be verbalized? Perhaps the answer is that the overt expression of the matter really exposes its true nature. To know that a person is thinking about himself in this way would seem to be inappropriate to most people. What if Nels knew that his girlfriend was thinking those things? What if everyone suspected that George was reflecting on those sentiments? What would be the reaction? Very likely most people would view it as pride.

Some may suggest that that reaction is just a reflection of our culture. That is, Christianity and other forces have promoted an anti-self-esteem attitude. But serious consideration needs to be given to the possibility that pride may actually be involved, and regardless of how we seek to justify it with self-theory in the daylight of reality it shows up for what it really is. Of course, books on self-love, both secular and evangelical, are filled with assurances that self-love is not pride. Their defensiveness on that point may be an unintentional recognition of the fact that, until recent years, that was a widespread attitude both among the general public and in the church.

That negative reaction can be seen in William James's statement of the case. The reader will recall that we equated the category he called "self-feelings" with the "self-love" of contemporary spokesmen. One of the synonyms he used to describe positive self-feelings was "self-esteem," a term prevalent in today's self-theory literature. Along with self-esteem James used a number of terms that have a negative connotation to describe positive self-feelings—terms such as "pride, conceit, vanity, arrogance, and vain-glory." On the other hand, to describe negative self-feelings James spoke of "modesty, humility, confusion, diffidence, shame, mortification, contrition, the sense of obloquy, and personal despair." Some of those synonyms would be viewed as favorable from a biblical perspective and some would not, but it appears that James saw the man with high self-feelings as proud, and the one with low self-feelings as humble.

The discrepancy between James's evaluation and that of contemporary writers is not that they are referring to a different phenomenon, but rather that they are evaluating it differently from an ethical point of view. James, writing a decade before the turn of the century, was reflecting the attitude of his time toward a person who felt good about himself. However, in the existential atmosphere of the contemporary scene the person who does *not* feel good about himself is the social misfit.

THE BIBLICAL CONTEXT

The question then arises, Which one is right? We have seen that Scripture has spoken clearly on the subject. Consider again 2 Timothy 3:1-5. The term "difficult times" means seasons or periods of time characterized by the fact that they are hard to take, troublesome, harsh, or fierce. The factors that will cause those times to be so hard are the sins contained in the following list given by Paul, a list that begins with "lovers of self." We demonstrated that the Greek word used here is a compound made up of the word "self" plus *philia*, the type of love described by contemporary self-theory, a feeling type of love.

Paul depicts that self-love as a serious peril. It is not only a characteristic of the last days, but apparently Paul sees it as the leading one, of which the other sins on the list may be by-products. We will examine that possibility more closely later.

What specifically is the essence of self-love? We have suggested that it is pride. Why then do we find pride ("arrogant") also listed in the passage (v. 2)? There are several words in the Greek New Testament that convey the idea of pride, and each one carries a somewhat different emphasis. The word in 2 Timothy 3:2 has in view the person who sees himself as above someone else. Whether self-love leads to that is a question to be dealt with later, but that particular manifestation is not at the heart of the matter of self-love.

What then is the central feature of pride? One writer indicates that its essence is man's refusal to depend on God, but rather "... to attribute to self the honor due to Him. ..." It is interesting to note that in the view of Greek philosophers pride was regarded as a virtue and humility as a vice.[1]

1. D. H. Tongue, "Pride" *The New Bible Dictionary*, ed. J. D. Douglas (Grand Rapids: Eerdmans, 1962), p. 1027.

As we look at two definitions of the opposite quality, humility, we find the same issue in view, the need for man to give to God the honor due Him. Vernon Grounds describes humility as

> . . . the proper attitude of the human creature toward his divine creator. It is the spontaneous recognition of the creature's absolute dependence on the Creator, an ungrudging, unhypocritical acknowledgment of the guilt which separates Self-subsistent Being from utterly contingent being, Kierkegaard's "infinite qualitative difference between God and man." It is the bent-knee stance of awed and grateful awareness that existence is a gift of grace, that inscrutable mercy which, having called a person out of non-being, sustains him moment by moment from lapsing back into nothingness. Humility, then, is explicated in Abraham's confession that he is but "dust and ashes" (Gen. 18:27). It is explicated again in Paul's sharp reminder to the inflated Corinthians that man's position before God is necessarily that of a recipient, a beggar whose hands are empty until divine benevolence fills them (I Cor. 4:6, 7).[2]

Another has described it succinctly as an acknowledgment by the believer ". . . that all he has and is he owes to the Triune God who is dynamically operative on his behalf. He then willingly submits himself under the hand of God (Jas. 4:6-10; 1 Pet. 5:5-7). Thus humility should not be equated with a pious inferiority complex. It can be pretended on the part of false teachers (Col. 2:18, 23) in acts of self-abasement."[3]

Throughout evangelical writings on self-love we have found an ambivalence arising from attempts to demon-

2. Vernon C. Grounds, "Humility," *The Zondervan Pictorial Encyclopedia of the Bible*, ed. Merrill C. Tenney, 5 vols. (Grand Rapids: Zondervan, 1975), 3:222.
3. Frederic R. Howe, "Humility," *Wycliffe Bible Encyclopedia*, ed. Charles F. Pfeiffer, Howard F. Vos, and John Rea, 2 vols. (Chicago: Moody, 1975), p. 821.

strate that man has autonomous worth and capacities while still trying to hold to the biblical teaching of his total dependence on God. That struggle evidences itself in statements such as the following: "The proper Christian self-image . . . does not imply pride in ourselves but rather glorying in what Christ has done and continues to do for us."[4] But if it is Christ who has done and continues to do everything for us, why should we not turn the focus from ourselves as recipients of His grace to Christ Himself? In this and other examples that could be gleaned there is one common error—the attempt, to one degree or another, to assign to man the esteem that is rightfully God's.

Once we understand self-love basically as pride we note that the Scriptures speak to the problem in various ways. We see self-love in the story of the tax-gatherer and the Pharisee in Luke 18:9-14. If self-love advocates would seek to disclaim association with the Pharisee, they certainly could not relate to the publican. We also see the rejection of self-love at the very outset of the beautitudes in the words "Blessed are the poor in spirit" (Matthew 5:3). That utterance of our Lord is not compatible with a high sense of self-esteem. The Bible also contains direct statements such as Proverbs 25:27: "It is not good to eat much honey, nor is it glory to search out one's own glory," or Proverbs 27:2: "Let another praise you, and not your own mouth, a stranger and not your own lips."

Do secular self-theorists also attempt to deny that their concept of self-love manifests itself as pride? There we seem to be at something of an impasse. James viewed positive self-feelings or self-esteem as pride, but contemporary self-theory views them favorably. James may have been biased by the Christian influence of his era, but then contemporary self-theorists may be under the sway of existentialism.

4. Anthony A. Hoekema, *The Christian Looks at Himself* (Grand Rapids: Eerdmans, 1975), p. 57.

ADLER'S THEORY OF INFERIORITY

To understand this dichotomy in secular thinking we need to look at a key theorist, a neo-Freudian named Alfred Adler. Adler's theory of personality revolved around the idea that *all* people experience inferiority feelings. He wrote, "To be a human being means to feel oneself inferior."[5] As a result, he saw the major goal of personality to be the establishment of superiority, not in the sense of seeking to be better than someone else, but rather the reaching of some sort of perfection (a distinction most self-theorists seek to hold).

That line of reasoning holds a very significant hidden implication, however. If to be human means to feel oneself inferior, then superiority feelings of the wrong kind (pride) logically are eliminated as an aspect of humanness. One result of that type of thinking is the "diagnosis" we often hear when someone is acting in a proud way: "He is just trying to cover up his inferiority complex." It seems to be a nice way to give people the benefit of the doubt, to let them off the hook where pride is concerned. (The problem of course is that the Bible speaks of pride as a genuine problem and not just as a facade to hide inferiority. In fact, we read little in Scripture about inferiority being a problem, but a great deal is said about the sin of pride.)

We can understand why Adler's theory would be received enthusiastically by modern psychology, because it does away with the problem of human pride. This may be why psychologists such as Fromm and Rogers are so concerned about people developing self-esteem, but appear not to be bothered by people who esteem themselves too highly. This same one-sided emphasis is found among evangelical self-theorists despite the biblical cautions against excessive pride. Those writers seem to show little or no anxiety that

5. Duane Schultz, *Theories of Personality* (Monterey, Calif.: Brooks/ Cole, 1976), p. 51.

their encouragement to self-love may produce excessive pride.

MASLOW'S OBSERVATIONS

One contemporary psychologist who has built a significant data base for his conclusions is Abraham Maslow. Maslow, one of the founding fathers of humanistic psychology, includes self-esteem as one of the stages in his hierarchy of needs. Across the years he did a fascinating series of studies that were collected in a book entitled *Dominance, Self-Esteem, Self-Actualization*. Maslow believes self-esteem is related to dominance feelings. For example, in one study he describes dominance feelings with synonyms such as "self-esteem, self-confidence, and high self-respect." These seem to be the same concepts that Rogers and evangelical self-theorists have in view when they speak of self-esteem or self-love.[6]

According to Maslow, when two people enter a relationship the one with the higher dominance feelings will assume what he calls "dominance." The other will be in a subordinate status. Using the example of a marriage in which the wife has the dominance he observes that ". . . she is more confident in her behavior, gets what she wants more often than does the husband, feels superior to him, generally feels herself to be stronger than he is, and respects herself more than she does him."[7]

Notice what Maslow is saying here. His observations indicate that a high sense of self-esteem tends to make a person superior to and respect himself more than a person with lower self-esteem, which often results in the former getting his way with the latter. Maslow developed that concept after extensive and careful observation, so his con-

6. Richard J. Lowry, ed., *Dominance, Self-Esteem, Self-Actualization: Germinal Papers of A. H. Maslow* (Monterey, Calif.: Brooks/Cole, 1973), pp. 106-7.
7. Ibid., p. 50.

clusions may be more trustworthy than the more speculative ones of men like Erich Fromm.

In citing Maslow we certainly are not suggesting that he
would use those conclusions as we would; he is not speaking
to the moral, and definitely not to the biblical, implications
of his findings. It is interesting, however, that though he is
basically a humanistic psychologist his views on self-esteem
are substantially different from those of Rogers.

Maslow's findings indicate that high self-esteem generates a basic feeling of superiority. Moreover, it is not the
innocent superiority Adler described but one that definitely
carries connotations of pride and tends to lead toward selfishness.

Maslow's observations help to explode the myth of self-
theory, both secular and evangelical, that as I feel good
about myself I naturally will seek to be a blessing to others
because I have been freed from my low self-esteem. It
seems logical that a person who is very pleased with himself will in turn seek to please himself. In realistic terms,
this is what we find to be true in daily experience. The kind
of self-love encouraged by self-theory (*philia*) leads to an
excessive self-concern in which the person does not love
(*agapē*) his neighbor, in the volition and action sense, *as* he
loves himself but *less than* he loves himself. We remember
that the *agapē* self-love of the neighbor passage is part of
man's natural makeup. As such it must be kept in check so
that it does not neglect the interests of our neighbor. But
when self-love puts self before neighbor, that is selfishness
and therefore sin. We cannot separate self-theory from its
existential base, which includes excessive self-love.

THE "ME" GENERATION

Paul Vitz directly links the "me" orientation of our society with the teachings of self-theory. In establishing this
link he cites as examples advertisement copy such as the
following from *Psychology Today* magazine: "I LOVE ME.

I am not conceited. I'm just a good friend to myself. And I like to do whatever makes me feel good. . . ."[8]Here is the usual disclaimer that self-love does not involve pride. But the fact is that self-esteem does not lead to ministry to others, but ministry to self. The assertion to the contrary appears to be a rather empty justification for loving ourselves. Perhaps it may be argued that a person with a terrible self-image cannot help society because he is too occupied with his own problems. Although that may be true, it does not answer the objections raised against excessive self-love. It is like arguing that the man who spends all day in a health club lifting weights and then admiring his physique can do many more good things for others than the person in the hospital bed. That commits the logical fallacy of seeking to prove that one extreme is right by showing that the other is wrong. It also assumes that the only two options available are a very good self-image or a very bad self-image.

Vitz's conclusion is further substantiated by the fact that the popularization of self-love has been followed immediately by best sellers such as *Looking Out for Number One* and a major emphasis on self-assertion, the latest rage in secular psychology. Such developments following hard on the heels of the embracing of self-love demonstrate that an attitude of superiority and all that goes with it is at the heart of self-love, despite disclaimers to the contrary.

We must conclude that the modern self-love movement actually has produced many distasteful by-products. Returning to 2 Timothy 3, it takes little imagination to see how items on that list—such as greed, boasting, pride, love of pleasure more than love of God, and so on—could be outgrowths of self-love. But the greatest peril of self-love is demonstrated for us perhaps inadvertently by Robert Schuller in his definition of self-love. "It is a divine aware-

8. Paul Vitz, *Psychology as Religion: The Cult of Self Worship* (Grand Rapids: Eerdmans, 1977), pp. 57, 62.

ness of personal dignity. It is what the Greeks called reverence for the self. It is an abiding faith in yourself. It is a sincere belief in yourself."[9] Divine awareness, reverence, faith, and belief are all words with strong religious connotations (a point that Vitz makes candidly in *Psychology as Religion: The Cult of Self-Worship*). The greatest peril of self-love is that it is worship of self. It is idolatry with self as the idol, the antithesis of the legitimate blessedness that comes from being poor in spirit. It leads to pride toward God and selfishness.

So we must ask some obvious questions. If self-esteem is not biblical, what then? If it is pride to love self, should we seek to deprecate ourselves? Are *those* the only two alternatives? That seems to be the assumption of virtually all self-theory. But we believe the Scripture teaches a remarkably simple and refreshing third alternative.

9. Robert Schuller, *Self-Love: Dynamic Force of Success* (New York: Hawthorne Books, Inc., 1969), p. 32.

13

A Biblical Alternative

We need to recognize that at least on one point self-theory has laid a valid emphasis. From a biblical perspective we cannot imagine that God has planned a life of self-castigation for us. A "Woe is me" attitude hardly need characterize our daily lives.

We could conclude the same from a human standpoint as well. A person who lives in constant awareness of failure and guilt probably is not going to be an effective spouse, parent, neighbor, or a fruitful Christian.

Because a deep awareness of low self-esteem is so devastating we can understand why many people in that situation have looked to self-love as a welcome alternative. And from a human point of view, it is; a person with high self-esteem can fight his way through life more successfully and with less trauma then one with low self-esteem. Given that fact, it is little wonder that self-theory has become so popular in secular and Christian circles. It also is not surprising that converts in both camps say, "I know it works. It has helped me." No doubt it has, in the sense that the old problems of inferiority, fearfulness, and being dominated are gone, or at least are not as acute.

The question is, though, whether that is God's way of getting through life. Is that His answer to low self-esteem? It is doubtful whether we have solved the problem or

131

merely exchanged symptoms. In medicine some "cures" produce side effects almost as detrimental as the disease itself. Excessive self-love may be as bad or worse than low self-esteem, but the symptoms are more compatible with our society and so are not as evident because of the value system we have adopted.

We have suggested that 2 Timothy 3:1-5 is in fact a list of some by-products of self-love. From a biblical standpoint those things are a cause for alarm, but we must realize that they probably are not considered to be all that bad by our society. Many are accepted and even embraced.

Perhaps one of the reasons the Bible has so much to say about pride and so little to say about low self-esteem is that the person suffering from the latter feels the pain and is aware of his need for help, whereas the person living in pride is in a far more comfortable position. The proud assert themselves, dominate others, get what they want (at the expense of others if necessary), and then others exalt them out of fear and respect for their wealth and power.

So we admit that the proud person, the one with high self-esteem, does do better in this life, but he does so by using a method that is neither taught nor blessed by the Scriptures. However, we have concluded as well that a life of low self-esteem cannot be the answer. What then is that third alternative?

AN ALTERNATIVE TO SELF-LOVE

Perhaps a couple of opening illustrations will help us focus our thinking on this new topic. I shall never forget New Year's Day, 1978. The University of Arkansas Razorbacks had won a bid to the Orange Bowl football classic. To add to the excitement, the opponent was Oklahoma, an old and bitter rival. As if that was not enough, before the game several key Arkansas players were booted off the team for misconduct. A furor erupted, but the decision held firm. What started out as a great rivalry now became a "holy war" to determine whether it really did pay to do the right thing.

From the first snap of the ball Arkansas went on a tear, moving up and down the field almost at will. In the midst of all the excitement my sophisticated wife momentarily set aside her genteel Pennsylvania upbringing and began yelling instructions to the coach, players, and occasionally, to the referee. As I look back on the occasion perhaps the best way to describe her reaction is to say that she "forgot herself" completely.

It has always amazed me in my years of teaching homiletics that the straight-faced, dead-pan, rigid student putting everyone to sleep in the classroom is the same young man who the night before in the dormitory, with a ring of friends around him, was expounding in great homiletic form. What made the difference? In the classroom he was "self-conscious," but in the dorm he "forgot himself."

Now I am not talking about a person throwing out all restraint and allowing his instincts to drive him where they will. I am referring to the focus of the mind. My wife was absorbed totally in the game. The student in the dorm was concentrating on his message to his friends. But what happened in the classroom? With all eyes focused on him, he began to ask himself some questions. "How do I look?" "Do they like me?" "Will I remember what comes next?" "How are my gestures?" He became what we call self-conscious.

The point is that it is possible for a person to "lose himself" in what he is doing. Is that good or bad? In the student's case it was good, because as he lost his self-concern his personality and natural vibrancy surfaced.

The situations described above illustrate in a limited way the alternative to self-love we are suggesting. We believe the biblical alternative to the wave of concern over self-image is have *no self-image at all*. Underlying that approach is the fact that both self-love and self-hate are self-centered attitudes. As we shall see, that inward focus is

destructive in nature, whereas a focus on others is productive. By changing the direction of our emotional occupation
from inward to outward we alleviate the destructive results
of self-centered emotions and realize the blessings of a
preoccupation with others.

Now if this kind of experience that happens to all of us on
occasion was to become the *pattern* of one's life; if his involvement with and concern for others was so intense that
he "forgot himself"; if even his daily work was done so
wholeheartedly that he was not aware of himself; if when
the work was finished he became "lost" in communion with
the Lord; *then* he could cease worrying about his self-
image. In effect he would have none! The goal is to focus on
others, and the negative qualities of both low and high
self-esteem will disappear.

But it is fair to ask if such a goal can be achieved. Is it
unrealistic even to suggest it? We think not, because as we
shall see the Bible calls us to an other-oriented way of
living, a life whose total focus is the Lord, others, and that
which the Lord has called us to do.

To help clarify what we mean here we should specify
what we do *not* mean by other-oriented living, or excluding
self-image from our awareness. First, we are not advocat-
ing the elimination of all self-evaluation. That is a vital
aspect of life. In Romans 12:3, a much misunderstood
verse, Paul calls us to evaluate our capacities for service
(not to feel good about ourselves). We *need* to evaluate our
performance for the purpose of managing our lives effectively for the Lord.

But as William James pointed out, there is an important
distinction between that type of evaluation and self-feelings
or self-esteem. Self-evaluation is more of an objective process whereas self-esteem is almost exclusively subjective.
The former looks at our level of competency in a given area
or how well we have performed a given task. The latter has
to do with our worth or status. James said those were

distinct categories and not necessarily related.

In addition when we speak of other-oriented living we are not talking about the elimination of self-image altogether but the elimination of self-image *from our awareness*. For example, let us assume that when he thinks about himself a person has a tendency toward negative self-feelings. We are not necessarily talking about either trying to deny or change that tendency. Rather, our goal is an outward focus so that the negative tendency is not activated habitually.

It should be obvious already that the approach suggested above is quite different from that usually offered by self-theory. Hoekema is typical of that approach when he observes that "it requires a pretty healthy kind of self-esteem for us to be more concerned for the other man's honor than for our own."[1] In other words, the person with low self-esteem must raise it considerably before he can expect to minister to others.

But we must challenge that conclusion on at least two counts. First, there is no scriptural warrant for the kind of cause/effect relationship suggested above. Also, it is questionable how much self-theory actually can change a person's self-esteem. Some psychologists have concluded that showing a person he has no objective basis for a poor self-image does not substantially change his view of himself.

The question of the practicality of the other-oriented approach to daily living has been raised already. We admit readily that it is one of the most difficult things we can do, and one that demands the power of the indwelling Holy Spirit to accomplish. It may even seem that the goal is an impossibility, and perhaps in the absolute sense it is. But we could say the same about the whole Christian life. However, that is never a valid reason for giving up on the "good fight" of faith.

1. Anthony A. Hoekema, *The Christian Looks at Himself* (Grand Rapids: Eerdmans, 1975), p. 78.

We need to remember that in any given situation we do not *have* to sin. God can give us the power to overcome the obstacle or temptation, and He can do it again and again. The ideal of other-oriented living can be approached in the same way. If it is possible at this moment, then it is possible in the next as well. What is more, the human impossibility of the task is no stumbling block, because God has already called us to a humanly impossible life!

14

The Evidence from Scripture, Part 1

We come now to consider the matter of biblical support for our alternative to self-love. If we can see some indicators, some signposts that tell us we are on the right road, then we are on solid ground to undertake an in-depth treatment of the subject.

SOME BIBLICAL SIGNPOSTS

One such indicator is the absence of any positive teaching on the subject of self-love, which we have pointed out frequently. Of course, that in itself is not sufficient evidence to support our thesis, but nonetheless it is worth noting once more. It is at least a strong encouragement to look further.

A second argument is that other-oriented living is the only reasonable option left to us. Excessive self-love is condemned in 2 Timothy 3, and although we have seen some biblical reasons why we might have a bad self-image, the Bible does not teach that God wants us living under the constant cloud of our failures and the scars they leave. Therefore, we conclude that the only biblical option is to rid our focus of self-image altogether.

We find another signpost in our Lord's teaching on judging others in the Sermon on the Mount. Jesus said, "Do not judge lest you be judged yourselves" (Matthew 7:1). But later on in the chapter He warns of false prophets who will be as wolves in sheep's clothing. But how are we to detect them? "You will know them by their fruits" (v. 16a). Those two ideas appear to be in conflict. How do we reconcile Matthew 7:1 with exhortations to judgment such as the one cited, or Matthew 18:15-17, or the example of Galatians 2:11, in which Paul blamed Peter for his duplicity?

The answer is that in Matthew 7:1 Jesus is not talking about the more objective matters referred to in the examples given above. Rather, He is concerned with the kind of subjective judgment illustrated earlier in His sermon: "Whoever shall say to his brother, 'Raca,' shall be guilty before the supreme court; and whoever shall say, 'You fool,' shall be guilty enough to go into the hell of fire" (Matthew 5:22b). It is not our prerogative to judge whether someone is empty-headed (Raca) or foolish, that is, make an overall evaluation of his worth.

We have already observed the need to evaluate our capacities and performance without having to render subjective judgments, good or bad, about our worth. That is what Paul seems to be saying in 1 Corinthians 4:3b: "In fact, I do not even examine myself." He further elaborates, "The one who examines me is the Lord" (v. 4b). Paul has been dealing with the problem of divided loyalties among the Corinthians, who were trying to determine the most worthy of their ministers and then identifying with him.

In verse 2 Paul acknowledges his responsibility to be faithful to his ministry, but then he asserts that any value judgment regarding it belongs to the Lord. That apparently was more than sufficient for him, for he felt no obligation to render a judgment. Certainly Paul evaluated the effectiveness of his ministry on many occasions, but that is different from saying, "I feel pretty good about myself. I give myself a good rating." On the contrary, Paul says, "I will leave that up to God."

It appears then that the biblical approach to judgment is consistent, whether we are judging ourselves or others.

Decisions regarding objective matters may be part of our responsibility to make, but any judgment regarding overall worth or esteem is the Lord's business.

Here is the solution to the problem of a poor self-image and frustration over missed opportunities and reward. We need to confess those sins and then leave the judgment of our reward in God's hands. As we seek to develop a positive self-image we will always be faced with some scars and loss. But if after confession we again turn our focus outward and upward, the question, "How well am I doing?" from a subjective (self-esteem) perspective will no longer be a concern. That does not rule out the same question in objective (action) areas. There is a clear distinction between those two self-orientations. In the first, we are evaluating *ourselves*. In the second, we are evaluating the effectiveness of *actions and programs* (our service).

An interesting feature of personality comes into play here regarding sin and confession. Frequently in counseling a person will loudly proclaim what a terrible person he or she is. But when asked what they have done wrong they become strangely quiet or avoid the question by returning to their former lament. Some counselees who are so willing to proclaim their wickedness become irate and angry when pressed to give concrete examples of their wrong-doings! To call yourself an "awful person" does not seem too bad because you are both to be pitied for your condition and praised for your nobility in admitting it.

But to confess sin is different. When we are faced with the specific wrongdoings and hurt we have done to others the sinfulness of sin becomes far more real. Also, confession carries with it both guilt and the need for restitution and change. So judging ourselves subjectively is of no help. It is often a detriment in that it can be a smoke screen to keep people from asking specific questions about their behavior.

Let us now consider still another indicator that would

suggest our intended course of action is biblically sound. Here we will move deeper into our subject as we come close to the heart of the issue.

One hermeneutical principle that some give credence to is the law of "first mention," that is, the first time a doctrine or subject is mentioned in the Bible is of particular importance and sets the tone for that topic throughout Scripture. That principle seems to hold true in enough instances to indicate that it may be valid. But whether we accept the principle, it is evident that in Genesis we find the seed-plot of many biblical concepts.

The first mention of self-consciousness in the Bible is found in Genesis 3:7-11. The context here is extremely significant. Verse 6 describes one of the most awesome events of history, the Fall of man. So Genesis 3:7 is the first recorded consequence of that tragic plunge into sin: "Then the eyes of both of them were opened, and they knew that they were naked." That this awareness of nakedness is crucial is indicated by the fact that it is the focal point of the verses under our consideration.

We may speculate about the garb of Adam and Eve prior to that moment. The key to the verse is that their eyes "were opened," emphasizing the sudden realization of their nakedness. It was not a matter of *becoming* naked but of *perceiving* that they were.

What was the immediate result in this change in their self-perception? It is easy for us to miss the point here by seeing their desire for coverings only as an attempt to hide their condition from each other. Although there must have been a disturbing new self-consciousness between them, the text bypasses that to emphasize that their awareness led to a much deeper concern. That conclusion is borne out in verse 10, in which Adam answers when God calls him, "I heard the sound of Thee in the garden, and I was afraid because I was naked; so I hid myself." Adam responded with the same self-consciousness before God that he had no doubt had with Eve.

Of special interest is his emotional reaction to that new self-awareness: "I was afraid." The first fear man ever knew was tied directly to an enlarged self-awareness. What had that first couple enjoyed that now was lost? Obviously, prior to the Fall they were not aware of their nakedness in the sense that they were not self-conscious about it. Their attention had not been drawn to their own condition.

In the total lack of selfishness in that pristine setting the need to ask themselves about their self-esteem apparently had not arisen. So there was no need to respond in fear or defensiveness, or to boost and protect the image that would have been created by this self-reflection. The totally other-centered outlook had precluded the need to establish a self-image. Their interest was in each other and in the things about them in God's universe. Their focus also was on the Lord who made and fellowshipped with them, and it is instructive that the coming of sin brought with it a definite change in that focus.

It is fascinating to observe that God's design of the body supports that approach to life. He created us in such a way that we normally are not the object of our own attention. Of course we can see different parts of our bodies, but those do not give us a picture of ourselves or usually attract our attention. To really see what we look like we need a mirror. God's design gives us an outward focus. It requires human engineering and effort for us to look back at ourselves. So also it appears that God's spiritual design for man was to look upward and outward, not inward. Genesis 3:7-11 indicates that man's self-focus was a result of the Fall.

The Esteem Game

So we see a treadmill produced by sin. Sin creates guilt, resulting in self-consciousness, which leads to a self-centeredness that produces barriers (such as Adam's clothing and attempt to hide from God) and more sin. The added sin no doubt adds to the self-consciousness, and so the downward spiral goes.

What have been the human solutions to that dilemma? The first, seen above, is isolation and separation. Erecting barriers has always been typical of man. We seek to hide from others (and from God) if we can, but often we are thrown into situations where we cannot escape intimate contact with people. Whether we like it or not John Donne was right—no man is an island.

What happens in those cases? We fall back to our second line of defense. When the circumstances of life prevent us from hiding, our desire is to rid ourselves of the pain of self-consciousness, to seek to develop good feelings about ourselves, to pump up our self-regard. As we saw, Alfred Adler proposed that all people have inferiority feelings that cause them to strive for superiority. Adler's positive view of man led him to conclude that the striving was not the desire to get ahead of someone else, but rather a striving for a standard of self-perfection. However, history and society demonstrate that that is not true. Man *does* strive in a competitive way, individuals and societies do *not* seek merely to perfect themselves, but to subdue their neighbors, to win at all costs.

All of us feel the pressure of being drawn into the varying self-esteem games of our particular place in life and stratum of society. With some it involves buying a house they cannot afford so people will think they can. With others it means using drugs to show that they are "with it." There are clothing, cars, and a million status symbols large and small. With others, esteem is sought by the self-righteousness found in being a model citizen or in philanthropic endeavors.

In that competition for esteem some are winners, but of course some must lose. Those who have been born into the right circumstances, have the necessary abilities, receive sufficient attention and praise, and achieve a good position come out on top. They develop sufficient esteem to face their society relatively free from fear. They have resolved the problem that began with Adam in a self-centered way. But the losers live under the shadow of fear and shame. The "name of the game" is to be a winner, one of Maslow's high dominance types.

But a closer look at the winners reveals a problem—no one ever ultimately wins. The classic example of that was King Saul. He was the logical choice to rule Israel; he stood head and shoulders above the people. Then he came face-to-face with Goliath, who was head and shoulders taller than he, and day after day he hid in his tent. That is the way self-esteem works. There is always the need to keep climbing, always the fear that Goliath will come along. For the president there is always another election, and Caesar has to worry about Brutus. It is always embarrassing to be second, especially when you were once first.

DRAWING CONCLUSIONS

At this point we must differ with self-theorists on at least three counts. They postulate a group of people who have arrived in the area of self-esteem so that they no longer feel the need to play the games we have described above. They feel comfortable with themselves and with others.

We could question that conclusion, however. One problem is that we meet few, if any, people who seem to be in that category, even among Christians. Even the ones who at first glance seem to qualify often prove to be no different than other people on this count. We certainly are not criticizing those people but simply are saying that they feel the same pressures, have the same temptations, and display the same needs in regard to self-esteem.

A second difficulty with that hypothesis is that we do not find the Scriptures teaching that solution to the self-esteem problem or saying that anyone has "arrived." We must conclude that such a class of people does not exist. By nature we are all seeking to deal with dilemma.

That leads us to a second problem with self-theorists, one

we have dealt with before. They invariably seek to demonstrate that people with *high* self-esteem are not proud, but that it is the ones with *low* esteem who are really the proud ones. The logic involved in such a conclusion has been examined already. But they have a point in that low esteem *is* a manifestation of man's self-centeredness, just as is high self-esteem. The one results in fear and the other in pride.

A third difficulty with self-theory involves what we are to do with those who exhibit low self-esteem, the ones who are losing the esteem game. Offering them only unconditional acceptance seems tantamount to saying (using football terminology for the moment), "Even though you only moved the ball to your own ten-yard line, we'll just move the goalposts so you won't feel so bad"!

In other words, it is telling people that esteem is not performance-related, when in fact it is. The psychologist's office may be the only place where winning does not count. The problem is that sooner or later the client must walk out the front door, where he finds that there *are* conditions to acceptance. We realize self-theory postulates that by that time the person has sufficient esteem to withstand those assaults. But even assuming the therapy worked, what has been accomplished? He has replaced his fear with pride. Now, instead of seeking to hide he will seek situations in which people will be available to boost his esteem.

So humanity may be divided into two groups. The first (we will call them introverts) contains people who are losing the esteem game and, like Adam, their self-centeredness results in fear and hiding. The second group is the extroverts, those who have high self-esteem and whose self-centeredness is expressed in pride.

All of us gravitate toward one of those groups for various reasons. Most of us manage to keep our tendencies within socially acceptable limits. Extreme extroverts are labeled even by society as being "proud," whereas extreme introverts are "strange" or "withdrawn." Both extremes are socially unacceptable.

The solution to the human dilemma was initiated by God, who offered His Son, the Lord Jesus Christ, as our substitute, to die in our place for our sin. God has also sent His Holy Spirit to convict us of our sinful condition and alienation from God and to show us our desperate need for the forgiveness found in Christ. We must respond by admitting our guilt and need for God's forgiveness. By an act of faith we can receive God's gift of forgiveness and have new, abundant life in Christ.

That release from guilt is the first step on our way to other-oriented living. We also need cleansing from the defilement of daily living through sincere confession of sin (1 John 1:9). Sin will quickly shift our focus inward if allowed to go unconfessed. Freedom from the guilt and power of sin helps prepare us to live with an upward and outward focus.

15

The Evidence from Scripture, Part 2

Since we found self-consciousness to be a direct result of the Fall in Genesis 3, we should expect to find the concept of other-oriented living in the positive teaching of Scripture, and so we do. The core of Old Testament theology is in Deuteronomy 6:4: "Hear, O Israel! The LORD is our God, the LORD is one!" God is the self-existent, autonomous One who therefore is the source of all else. All is dependent on Him.

OUR LOVE FOR GOD

In view of who God is declared to be in Deuteronomy 6:4, we are given the only reasonable response in the next verse. "And you shall love the LORD your God with all your heart and with all your soul and with all your might." Our whole being is to be employed in worshiping and serving Him. Here is a totally God-centered orientation. Life consists not in looking inward and feeling good, bad, or otherwise about self. Rather, it centers on God, who is to inspire our awe. This mandate is repeated in all three of the synoptic gospels (Matthew 22:37; Mark 12:30; Luke 10:27).

The word "love" here is the Hebrew *aheb* that we studied in chapter 4. We concluded there that the term pertains primarily to will and action. Therefore the command does not center on how we feel toward God, though that may be involved. Rather it calls for the dedication of all our capacities to the Lord for the use that He ordains. That use, in brief, is to bring glory to Him by the ordering of our lives as He directs.

This is nothing less than a call for the total occupation of the human personality with God. Because the command originates in Deuteronomy, a legislative portion of Scripture, we should expect that God intends it to be taken literally. It is not an ethereal concept given for the purpose of theological discussion. It is an expression of God's just due based on who He is, and of His requirement that men reflect their recognition of Him by their actions.

That same sentiment is expressed by the apostle Paul in 1 Corinthians 6:19-20: "Or do you not know . . . you are not your own? For you have been bought with a price; therefore glorify God in your body." All of the energies of life are to be expended in bringing glory to Him.

OUR LOVE FOR OTHERS

A superficial understanding of the concept laid out above may lead a person to take up the life of a hermit in the middle of the desert or on top of a mountain, seeking to worship God alone. But when we see how Christ dealt with the command in the gospels it becomes apparent that just the opposite is required. With the command to love the Lord He linked Leviticus 19:18, the requirement to love our neighbor as ourselves.

Of that dual mandate to love God and neighbor Christ states, "On these two commandments depend the whole Law and the Prophets" (Matthew 22:40). The first requirement seems to summarize the first part of the Decalogue, which emphasizes our obligations toward God, and the second reflects the latter portion of the Ten Commandments, which involves our dealings with our neighbors.

It is significant that Christ designates specifically a first and a second commandment, because the order is absolutely necessary. One reason for that is that to view love of neighbor before or apart from love for God is mere humanism. But how can we love our neighbor if all of our energies—heart, soul, strength, and mind—are to be occupied with loving the Lord? (Remember we are defining love not in emotional terms by which we could claim to love everyone, but in the *agapē* sense of will and action, which calls for the expending of ourselves and our resources.)

The answer lies in the phrase "And a second is like it," (Matthew 22:39). How is the second command like the first? We answer, How do we love God? What do we do for Him? What can we give Him? There are some things we can do directly for God. Worship is one, perhaps the only one. But the majority of what we do for God involves loving our neighbor for His sake and to His glory.

Therefore, the second command is like the first in that it is part and parcel of carrying out the first commandment. God does not need anything from us, but we express our love for Him by keeping His commandment to love our neighbor. For example, we may say that we give a certain percentage of our income to the Lord. Of course, it is not given to Him in a direct sense, but indirectly as it is invested in His work of reaching our lost neighbors.

This brings us to the matter of loving our neighbor *as* ourselves. Already we have seen that an *agapē* type of love has as its focus the will and actions. Emotional self-love is not in view. Here we are commanded to be as sensitive to the needs of our neighbor as we are to our own, and to be as ready to do those things necessary to meet our neighbor's needs as we are to meet our own. The emphasis on action is seen in Matthew 7:12, "Therefore whatever you want others to do for you, do so for them, for this is the Law and the Prophets."

Though the command to love neighbor *as* self is repeated a number of times in the New Testament, it is not the fullest expression of the Lord's expectations for the Christian. In John 13:34 a new commandment is given, that we love as Christ loved us. The love that Christ had for us is described in John 15:13, "Greater love has no one than this, that one lay down his life for his friends." Christ not only calls us to love our neighbor *as* ourself, but *more than* ourself, even to the point of total self-giving.

The implication in the Old Testament is that after I have given the Lord the required offering and after I have met my obligation to my neighbor, the rest was mine to enjoy, to use to meet my needs and wants. However, it seems that in the New Testament even *agapē* self-love is eliminated in the call to love neighbor more than self. Of course that does not mean that we do not eat or clothe ourselves or meet other personal needs. But it does mean that our ultimate objective in so doing is not self-satisfaction but ministry to others.

This is what Paul is saying about his own ministry in 1 Corinthians 9:19: "For though I am free from all men, I have made myself a slave to all, that I might win the more." Paul had voluntarily given up all rights to *agapē* self-love in order to maximize his ministry to others. The New Testament not only excludes *philia* self-love, but in this sense *agapē* self-love is excluded as well. So the thrust of New Testament living is upward and outward, focused on others. Perhaps the best description of that is other-oriented living.

16

The Benefits of Other-Oriented Living

Other-oriented living is at once a most blessed and a most costly life-style. We recognize that self-theorists are seeking to solve some very real problems, particularly the feeling of inferiority and all that goes with it. We have found, however, that their solution merely transfers the person to a less painful but more dangerous condition, excessive self-love.

By way of contrast, an other-oriented life offers no remedies of that nature. It is not an easy solution. It begins with and continually demands death—death to self. Luke 9:23 tells us that that is to be our daily experience, and death hurts. The cross to be borne daily is that of self-denial. It is the rejection of self-oriented living so that our lives can be poured out in service to God and others.

Not surprisingly, a very crucial aspect of death to self is the area of self-feelings. Someone makes a negative comment about the job we are doing and our indignation toward that person begins to build, because self has been unjustly injured. If a second person makes a comment we may begin feeling sorry for ourselves. Let a third say something and we begin to feel depressed.

Or, if the comments are positive, we may begin to feel proud of ourselves rather than praise God, who gave us the capabilities and the strength and breath to use them.

151

Real discipline is needed to curb those self-feelings before they can do their detrimental work. To exercise that God-given discipline is a source of pain, part of dying to self.

But let us also consider the glorious fruits of an other-oriented approach to life. Those are legitimate, God-given, and contain no harmful side effects.

The Yoke of Christ

We read of one of those blessings in Matthew 11:28-30: "Come to Me, all who are weary and heavy-laden, and I will give you rest. Take My yoke upon you, and learn of Me, for I am gentle and humble in heart; and you shall find rest for your souls. For My yoke is easy, and My load is light."

When Jesus speaks of those who are "heavy-laden," we are reminded that one of the greatest loads we carry is our own self-esteem. Protecting the ego is a full-time job. We have noted the burden it creates of having constantly to maintain our self-image. Even the self-theorists have recognized this, and have sought a solution in the teaching of unconditional acceptance. But because that is not really a valid option, we are left with the burden of supporting our self-esteem through our own efforts.

Jesus said, "I will give you rest." It seems paradoxical that He gives rest by placing a different yoke on us. What is His yoke? The Lord tells us in the next verse. "For I am gentle and humble in heart." *That* is His yoke—the humility of selflessness, of not protecting our reputation, of not needing to make people realize who we are.

In addition to the burden of supporting our self-esteem there is also the load of fear. The introvert in his own way seeks to boost his esteem and the extrovert has his social fears. So we are all constantly fighting the battle, realizing that we could be done in by fear or loss of esteem at any time. Little wonder the passage uses such strong language for the fatigue resulting from such a load. But though it is lighter, we must take Christ's burden seriously. The choice is not whether we will bear a yoke. What a blessing it would be to us and others if each of us would exchange our yoke for Christ's!

William James recognized the psychological advantages of the selfless life when he observed:

> To give up pretensions is as blessed a relief as to get them gratified . . . The history of evangelical theology, with its conviction of sin, its self-despair, and its abandonment of salvation by works, is the deepest of possible examples. . . . There is the strangest lightness about the heart when one's nothingness in a particular line is once accepted in good faith.[1]

It is amazing that a psychologist such as James seems to grasp this scriptural principle more readily than do many evangelicals.

The rest that results from taking on the yoke of Christ applies not only to our moments of despair but to the mundane times in our circle of friends. Though we often do not realize it, those moments can be burdensome for many. Not that a real dread is experienced, but there is pressure to do what is necessary either to be accepted or to maintain the acceptance already won. The pressure sometimes is very real to perform, or in the case of the introvert, to hide.

How much better to approach those relationships with the thought, "I want to minister to you in some way today, whether by an encouraging word, word of exhortation, a smile that says I care about you, or by praying for you." If we can reproduce that attitude in every circumstance in which we are in contact with people, we will do away with the fear that comes from thinking about our-

1. William James, *The Varieties of Religious Experience: A Study in Human Nature* (New York: Longmans, Green, and Co., 1923), pp. 310-11.

selves. We will have rid ourselves of the need for esteem because we will have "lost ourselves" in ministry to others.

The value of that kind of experience has even been recognized by psychologist Abraham Maslow. Speaking of self-actualization, the highest form of fulfillment according to his theoretical construction, he explains:

> First, self-actualization means experiencing fully, vividly, selflessly, with full concentration and total absorption. It means experiencing without the self-consciousness of the adolescent. At this moment of experiencing, the person is wholly and fully human. This is a self-actualizing moment. This is a moment when the self is actualizing itself. As individuals, we all experience such moments occasionally. As counselors, we can help clients to experience them more often. We can encourage them to become totally absorbed in something and to forget their poses and their defenses and their shyness—to go at it "wholehog." From the outside, we can see that this can be a very sweet moment. In those youngsters who are trying to be very tough and cynical and sophisticated, we can see the recovery of some of the guilelessness of childhood; some of the innocence and sweetness of the face can come back as they devote themselves fully to a moment and throw themselves fully into the experiencing of it. The key word for this is "selflessly," and our youngsters suffer from too little selflessness and too much self-consciousness, self-awareness.[2]

Sigmund Freud recognized the same principle in his concept of being in love. In the following quote the "object" refers to that which the person loves: "The ego becomes more and more unassuming and modest, and the object more and more sublime and precious, until at last it gets possession of the entire self-love of the ego, whose self-sacrifice thus follows as a natural consequence. The ob-

2. A. H. Maslow, *The Farther Reaches of Human Nature* (New York: Viking, 1971), p. 45.

ject, so to speak, has consumed the ego."[3]

Here are the same basic factors discovered by Maslow. The person becomes so absorbed with the one he loves that self-sacrifice and ultimately the total consumption of the ego result.

FREEDOM FROM EMBARRASSMENT

The possibilities of this kind of life are exciting. How much richer and more genuine our personalities would be, and how much fuller our lives would become. In addition, an other-oriented approach would make some of the rough spots of life substantially easier. For example, one of the blessings of that mind-set is that it helps rid us of the pain of embarrassment. No one escapes embarrassing circumstances of varying degrees of severity. But when we have no *I* to protect, when it has been absorbed in others, there is no longer a firm basis for embarrassment.

INTERPERSONAL RELATIONS

Another area especially benefited by other-oriented living is that of difficult interpersonal relations. No one likes confrontations, whether at work, in the church, in marriage, business, or elsewhere. We may deal with them by building a head of steam and then approaching the person and letting it explode. But there are two problems with that option. First, it is an unscriptural methodology, and second, it seldom if ever accomplishes the goal. You may spend the rest of your life trying to pick up the pieces from your explosion.

Another popular approach is to avoid the problem. This is often done on the pious pretext that we will "let the Lord" deal with the problem. However, Scripture tells us there are occasions when the Lord has delegated that re-

3. Sigmund Freud, *The Standard Edition of the Complete Psychological Works of Sigmund Freud*, ed. and trans. James Strachey, 24 vols. (London: Hogarth, 1957), 18:113.

sponsibility to *us*. To renege is no more spiritual than to
say that we will allow the Lord to speak to our unsaved
neighbor.

But to approach a person about a problem in the right
way is a hard thing to do. To come to the other with a gentle
spirit, leaving yourself open to possible rejection, is a very
real form of dying to self. But as we shift our focus outward
we begin to see the person not as a problem but as someone
with real needs that we can attempt to minister to. That
does *not* mean the problem will not be dealt with, but
rather that it will be handled in the context of meeting the
needs of the other person. It may not remove all the fear
inherent at such times, but it can help turn a confrontation
into a vehicle for growth.

That selfless attitude also leaves us open to receive
criticism from the other person. We are not denying that
there may be an inward tendency to be defensive, but as we
discipline ourselves through the power of God to check
that urge, we can grow in our capacity to be open.

ABUNDANT LIFE

Still another blessing of other-oriented living is that it
leads to abundant life. To love God with all of our heart,
soul, strength, and mind means to live wholeheartedly.
We cannot overestimate the importance of vitality, of
spark, in the life of the Christian. Here is one place where
the children of this world often surpass the children of
light. We have every reason to sparkle, to be enthusiastic,
to work with zest. Life begets life.

But it may be objected, "That would be phony!" That's
just the problem! If we were meeting the demands of
agapē living it would be more real. Of course, personality
comes into play here. Some people seem to come by that
spark more naturally than others. But that does not mean
we are thereby relieved of our responsibility to develop the
needed quality of wholeheartedness in everything we do
for God and others.

TRUE CONFIDENCE

A final benefit of *agapē* living is that of true confidence. In the natural world our gifts never assure us of victory. So too in the Christian life it is not always God's will that we "win." Even in the midst of sincere ministry, such as singing, for example, we cannot be sure that our voice will not crack or that we will not forget the words. Perhaps the Lord wants us to demonstrate how to handle defeat and failure.

In the midst of such circumstances the confidence offered us by self-theory breaks down because it is based in ourselves. But our confidence in God can be real as we realize that despite the outcome we know that God's purposes are served and He is being glorified through it. That was Paul's testimony: "We are afflicted in every way, but not crushed; perplexed, but not despairing" (2 Corinthians 4:8). How could he say that? Look back at verse 7. It was because God had designed Paul's circumstances for *His* glory.

Other-oriented living has potential to remove the fears, the inhibitions, the need for games and pretensions, and other barriers in our relations with God and others. Then the life of God is free to flow through us to others. Some believe that all the aspects of the fruit of the Spirit (Galatians 5:22) are found in the first—*agapē*. It certainly is the starting point. It will draw your focus away from yourself to God and to others for His sake, and as you "lose" your life you will find it again in the presence of the One for whom you died to self—and began to live.

Moody Press, a ministry of the Moody Bible Institute, is designed for education, evangelization, and edification. If we may assist you in knowing more about Christ and the Christian life, please write us without obligation: Moody Press, c/o MLM, Chicago, Illinois 60610.